Brilliant guides

What you need to know and how to do it

When you're working on your computer and come up against a problem that you're unsure how to solve, or want to accomplish something that you aren't sure how to do, where do you look? Manuals and traditional training guides are usually too big and unwieldy and are intended to be used as end-to-end training resources, making it hard to get to the info you need right away without having to wade through pages of background information that you just don't need at that moment – and helplines are rarely that helpful!

Brilliant guides have been developed to allow you to find the info you need easily and without fuss and guide you through the task using a highly visual, step-by-step approach – providing exactly what you need to know when you need it!

Brilliant guides provide the quick easy-to-access information that you need, using a table of contents and troubleshooting guide to help you find exactly what you need to know, and then presenting each task in a visual manner. Numbered steps guide you through each task or problem, using numerous screenshots to illustrate each step. Added features include 'See also' boxes that point you to related tasks and information in the book, while 'Did you know?' sections alert you to relevant expert tips, tricks and advice to further expand your skills and knowledge.

In addition to covering all major office PC applications, and related computing subjects, the *Brilliant* series also contains titles that will help you in every aspect of your working life, such as writing the perfect CV, answering the toughest interview questions and moving on in your career.

Brilliant guides are the light at the end of the tunnel when you are faced with any minor or major task.

Publisher's acknowledgements

The author and publisher would like to thank the following for permission to reproduce the screen shots in this book:

Yahoo! UK, Google UK, Saga, Real and Yamaha Motor Co.

Microsoft product screen shots reprinted with permission from Microsoft Corporation. FujiFilm screen shots reprinted with permission from FujiFilm Electronic Imaging Ltd.

Every effort has been made to obtain necessary permission with reference to copyright material. In some instances we have been unable to trace the owners of copyright material, and we would appreciate any information that would enable us to do so.

Author's acknowledgements

The author would like to thank Karen, Sally and Andy for making this project so enjoyable.

About the author

P.K. MacBride spent 20 years at the chalkface in schools and technical colleges before leaving to work full-time as a writer, editor and typesetter. He has written over 100 books, mainly on computing topics, covering many aspects of computer programming, software applications and the Internet. He has been translated into over a dozen languages, including Russian, Portugese, Greek, Chinese and American.

Contents

Preface

The basic unit of computer memory is called a byte, but computers don't bite. And you can't do much damage to them either, whatever you do wrong – short of taking a hammer to them. The worst that can normally happen is that it will stop working, half-way through a job and that's easily solved – just turn it off and on again. For the most part, computer systems are logical, work in standard ways and follow the same set of basic rules. Once you understand those rules, you will be able to use your computer effectively, and tackle new applications confidently. This book will show you those rules. So, shed your fears. You can't break it, and it won't break you.

Being over 50 is no handicap when it comes to learning about computers. I'm over 50, though I've been using computers for 20-odd years, but I have many friends and relations who have come to computers, and mastered them, in their 50s, 60s, 70s and even 80s. We can all learn new things at any age. The biggest bar to learning is the belief that it will be difficult. Relax, using a computer is not difficult. (Designing a computer or developing new computer applications are, but no-one is asking you to do these things!)

Being over 50 may well, however, affect the sort of things that you want to learn about computers. If I had been writing this book for the under 50s, I would have included chapters on the full range of office applications: word processing, spreadsheets, databases and presentation software, because younger people may well need these to take their careers forward. Us older folks, if we are still in work, probably have all the IT skills we need for the job, and if we are now starting to learn about computers, it is for use in our leisure activities. We want to use them to write letters, minutes of meetings or our memoirs; create newsletters and posters for our clubs, store, edit, organise and print our digital photos and videos; get online and explore the internet. And that's what this book is about.

There are several different types of computer around, and lots of software. This book is for people who have a PC (of any make) running Windows Vista, perhaps with Word or Works as your word processor. Apart from that, all the software that is covered in this book is supplied as part of the Windows Vista package – and that is all most of us need.

P.K. MacBride, Southampton 2007

Introduction

i

Welcome to *Brilliant Computing for the Over 50s, Vista edition,* a visual quick reference book that shows you how to make the most of your PC. Focused specifically on the needs of those whose working life was not affected significantly by computers, it provides an introductory guide to using a computer. It will show you how to work in the Windows environment, organise your files, use a word processor, store and edit images from a camera, configure Windows to suit you, and will start you off exploring the Internet and communicating by email.

Find what you need to know – when you need it

You don't have to read this book in any particular order. We've designed the book so that you can jump in, get the information you need, and jump out. To find the information that you need, just look up the task in the table of contents or Troubleshooting guide, and turn to the page listed. Read the task introduction, follow the step-by-step instructions along with the illustration, and you're done.

How this book works

Each task is presented with step-by-step instructions in one column and screen illustrations in the other. This arrangement lets you focus on a single task without having to turn the pages too often.

How you'll learn

Find what you need to know – when you need it

How this book works

Step-by-step instructions

Troubleshooting guide

Spelling

Step-by-step instructions

This book provides concise step-by-step instructions that show you how to accomplish a task. Each set of instructions includes illustrations that directly correspond to the easy-to-read steps. Eye-catching text features provide additional helpful information in bite-sized chunks to help you work more efficiently or to teach you more in-depth information. The 'For your information' feature provides tips and techniques to help you work smarter, while the 'See also' cross-references lead you to other parts of the book containing related information about the task. Essential information is highlighted in 'Important' boxes that will ensure you don't miss any vital suggestions and advice.

Troubleshooting guide

This book offers quick and easy ways to diagnose and solve common problems that you might encounter using the Troubleshooting guide. The problems are grouped into categories that are presented alphabetically.

Spelling

We have used UK spelling conventions throughout this book. You may therefore notice some inconsistencies between the text and the software on your computer which is likely to have been developed in the USA. We have however adopted US spelling for the words 'disk' and 'program' as these are becoming commonly accepted throughout the world.

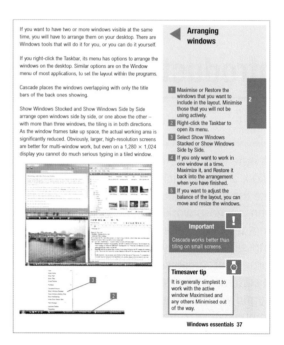

Instant computing

Introduction

Computing does not have to be difficult. You don't need a degree in Computer Science to produce a letter or the minutes of a meeting with a word processor, or to draw a picture or diagram on the screen. (Of course, you do need a degree in Computer Science, or something like it, if you are going to develop new software or design new equipment, but that's not what we're about here!) In this first chapter you will see how little you need to learn to be able to do useful things with your computer. We will explore three applications that are present in every Windows Vista computer:

- WordPad, a simple but effective word processor
- Windows Explorer, which is used for managing files
- Paint, a basic application for creating and editing images.

Important

Windows Vista allows its users to customise the screen in many ways. As a result, your screen may well not look exactly the same as the ones in the screenshots. You will see how to customise the display in Chapter 7.

Discovering your PC

A desktop PC system typically has these components:

Monitor or VDU (Visual Display Unit). On older desktop PCs this is similar to a TV, but most now have flat LCD screens. Newer monitors usually have 17-inch screens, capable of resolutions up to 1,600 × 1,200. (The resolution is the number of pixels – dots of light – that make up the screen.)

System unit – the box containing the 'works'. This may act as a base for the monitor, or stand beside it, as in the illustration, or on the floor beneath.

On the front you should be able to see the front panels of a floppy disk drive and a CD/DVD-ROM drive, and two buttons – one is the on/off button, the other the reset button.

At the back you will find a number of sockets and connections, most with cables plugged into them.

Inside, and best left to the experts, are the power supply, the CD/DVD-ROM, floppy disk and hard disk drives, and the main circuit board (the motherboard) containing the main processor, the memory and other chips; plus a sound card, graphics card, modem and other circuit boards.

Keyboard – though mainly for entering text and numbers, the keys can also be used for controlling software, as you will see.

Mouse – used for controlling the cursor on screen, allowing you to select items, start programs, draw pictures, and more.

There will also normally be speakers and a printer, and possibly a scanner, attached.

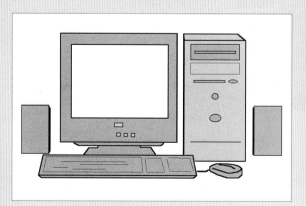

For your information

A portable or laptop PC is in practice the same as a desktop model, except that the screen is in the lid and the system unit is in the base of the keyboard. There will usually be some form of touch pad or mini-joystick in the keyboard to use in place of a mouse.

Windows is an operating system – and more. An operating system handles the interaction between the processor and the screen, memory, mouse, disk drives, printer and other equipment. It is a bridge between the hardware of the computer and the applications – such as word processing or spreadsheet programs. Whatever hardware you are using, if it has a version of Windows, it can run any application written for that or for earlier versions of Windows. (This book assumes that you are using Windows Vista – but if you have an earlier version, such as XP, the differences are not very great.)

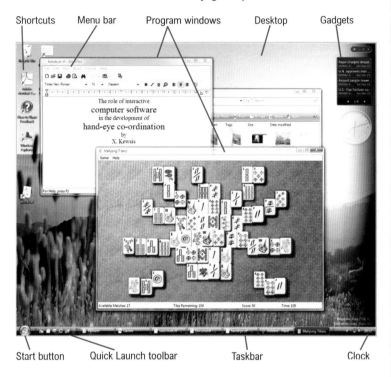

Shortcuts   Menu bar   Program windows   Desktop   Gadgets

Start button   Quick Launch toolbar   Taskbar   Clock

Shortcuts – instant access to programs. You can create shortcuts.
Menu bar – gives access to a program's commands.
Desktop – you can change the background picture or pattern and its colours.
Program windows – adjust their size and placing to suit yourself.
Start button – opens the Start menu, from where you should be able to start any program on your PC.
Quick Launch toolbar – a quick way to start key programs.
Taskbar – when a program is running, it has a button here. Click on a button to open its window and bring it to the front of the desktop.
Clock – optional, but handy.

Starting Windows

1

Start up

1 Turn on the PC.

2 If the monitor has its own switch, turn it on.

3 Various messages and images will appear to let you know that things are happening.

4 If you are on a network, you will need to log on – to enter your user name and password.

5 After a few more minutes' wait while the last files are loaded and the system configured for your use, the Desktop screen will appear.

Starting a program

The programs already on your PC, and virtually all of those that you install later, will have an entry in the All Programs part of the Start menu. Selecting one from here will run the program, ready for you to start work.

A program can also be run by selecting a document that was created by it. Links to the documents used most recently are stored in the Recent Items folder, which can also be opened from the Start menu.

Starting from Programs

1 Click .

2 Point to All Programs.

3 Click on the folder that contains the program – you may have to click on a sub-folder within it.

4 Click on the name to run the program.

Starting from documents

1 Click .

2 Point to Recent Items, on the middle right of the Start menu.

3 Click on the file to open it in the application that created it.

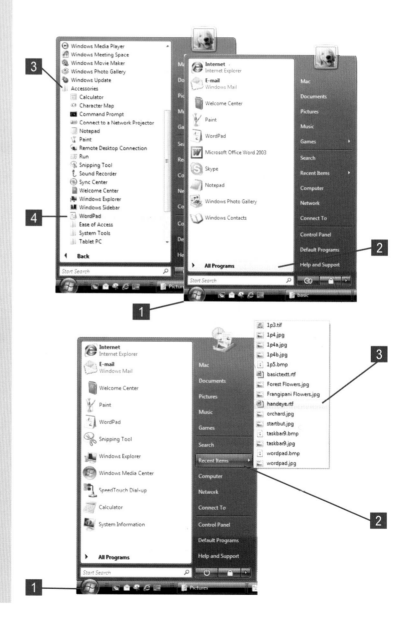

Word processing is one of the most popular uses of computers, and not surprising. Word processing puts well presented, neatly formatted, correctly spelled documents in the reach of everyone.

Windows Vista comes with its own word processor – WordPad. This does not have the full scope of a professional package, such as Word, but it has a good range of formatting facilities. You can set selected text in any font, size or colour, add emphasis with **bold**, *italics* and <u>underline</u>, indent paragraphs or set their alignment, and even insert pictures, clip art, charts and many other types of objects. WordPad has all you need for writing letters, essays, memos, reports and the like. Could you write a book on it? Possibly, as long as it had a simple layout and you were happy to create the contents list and index by hand.

Most of us, most of the time, use only a fraction of the facilities of full-blown word processors. It is often more efficient to use WordPad – because it is simpler, faster to load and to run, and faster to learn!

Start WordPad

1 Click .

2 Point to All Programs.

3 Click on the Accessories folder.

4 Click on WordPad.

! Important

The best way to learn is to play. As you read through the next few pages, use WordPad to write a letter, or make notes on what you are learning, or even start that novel! But don't take it seriously. Keep the focus on exploring WordPad, not on the content of the document.

Starting word processing (cont.)

Entering text

All word-processors have word wrap. Don't press [Enter] as you get close to the right margin. WordPad will sense when a word is going to go over the end of a line and wrap it round to the start of the next. The only time you should press [Enter] is at the end of a paragraph or to create a blank line. If you change the margins of the page or the size of the font, WordPad will shuffle the text to fit, word wrapping as it goes.

Selecting text

- A block of text – anything from a single character to the whole document – is selected when it is highlighted. Once selected the text can be formatted, copied, deleted or moved.

- The simplest way to select text is to drag the mouse pointer over it. Take care if some of the text is below the visible area, as the scrolling can run away with you!

- A good alternative is to click the insertion point into place at the start of the block you want to select, then hold down [Shift] and use the arrow keys to move the highlight to the end of the block.

- When setting alignment or indents, which can only apply to whole paragraphs, it is enough to place the insertion point – the flashing vertical line where you type – into the paragraph.

- Double-click anywhere in a word to select it.

- Triple-click anywhere in a paragraph to select it.

Deleting errors

To correct mistakes, press [Backspace] to remove the last character you typed, or select the unwanted text and press either [Backspace] or [Delete].

Important

One of the great things about Windows applications – especially those from Microsoft – is that they do the same jobs in the same way. Once you have learnt how to enter text, open or save a file, select a font or whatever, in one application, you will know how to do it in the next.

You can do formatting in two ways – either select existing text and apply the format to it, or set up the format and then start typing. Either way, the formats are selected in the same way.

Use the Formatting toolbar when you want to change one aspect of the formatting – just click on the appropriate button or select from the drop-down lists.

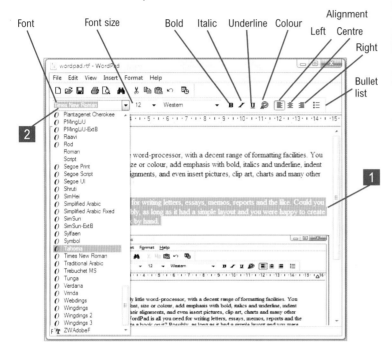

1 Select the text or go to where the new format is to start.

2 Use the Formatting tools.

Click on a button to apply or remove its formatting.

Or click the arrow beside the button to display its options and select one from the list or palette.

!

Important

Keep experimenting! Try to find a place to use every different type of formatting option.

Formatting with the Font dialogue box

Use the Font dialogue box when you want to define several aspects of the font at the same time, or if you want the rarely used strikeout effect.

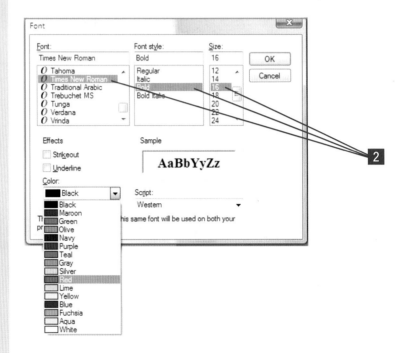

1 Select Font… from the Format menu.

2 Define the format and click OK .

Anything you type into WordPad – or most other applications – is lost when you close the application unless you save the document as a file on a disk.

The first time that you save a file, you have to specify where to put it and what to call it. If you then edit it and want to store it again, you can use a simple File, Save to resave it with the same name in the same place, overwriting the old file. If you edit a file and want to keep the old copy and the new one, then you can use File, Save As and save the new version under a different name.

In WordPad – again, as in many applications – you can save a file in several ways. The default is Rich Text Format, which can be read by most word processors and many other applications. You can also save the words, without the formatting, by using one of the text formats.

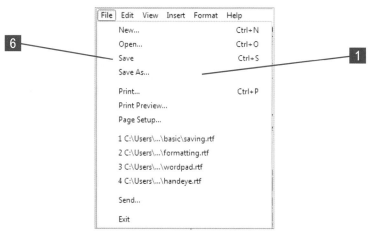

To save a new file

1 Open the File menu and select Save As…

2 The top left slot shows the folder that the file will be saved in. You can change this, but we won't bother with changing folders at this stage.

3 Type in a name to identify the file clearly.

4 Change the Save as type if necessary.

5 Click Save .

Resaving a file

6 Open the File menu and select Save.

or

7 Click Save on the toolbar.

Important

If you open a Word document in WordPad, you can save it again in Word format.

Closing and reopening files

Once a document has been saved as a file it can be reopened again whenever you want to add to it or edit it, or print out another copy. Just to prove this, we'll close the document – and close WordPad for good measure – then reopen it.

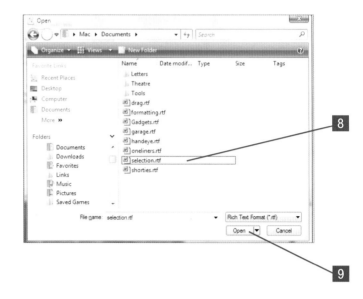

Close a file

1 Open the File menu and select New. This will close the file and clear the workspace ready for a new document.

Shut down WordPad

2 Open the File menu and select Exit or click ▭✕▭.

Restart WordPad

3 Click 🟦.

4 Point to All Programs.

5 Point to the Accessories folder.

6 Click on WordPad.

Open the file

7 Open the File menu and select Open.

8 Locate and select your file.

9 Click | Open ▾ |.

In almost every Windows application there are two ways to print a document:

Click the toolbar button to print one copy of the whole document, using the default printer.

Open the Print dialogue box to print selected pages, or set the number of copies, or control the quality of the printing.

Here's how printing works in WordPad. Use it to print your new file.

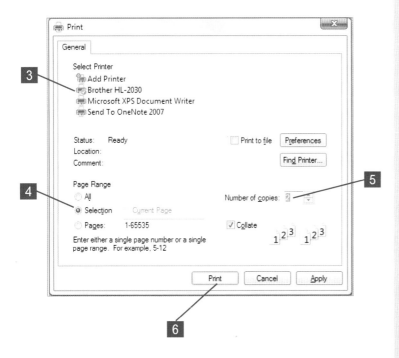

Print instantly

1 Check that the printer is on and that there is paper in it.

2 Click 🖨 .

Control the printout

1 If you only want to print part of the document, select it now.

2 Open the File menu and select Print... The Print dialogue box will open.

3 If you have a choice, select the printer.

4 In the Page Range area, choose what to print: the entire document, the part you selected earlier or a set of pages (type the number for a single page, or the first and last numbers, e.g. 3–5).

5 If you want more than one copy, enter how many.

6 Click [Print] .

Timesaver tip

If you only want the printout for your reference, click the Preference button to open a dialogue box where you can control the quality of the printing. Set it to Draft and the document will be printed about twice as fast as usual – and it will use less ink!

Managing files

Windows Explorer (or just Explorer for short) is the tool that we use for managing the files on our disks. You can start Explorer from Computer, Documents, Pictures and several other links on the Start menu – each opens Explorer at a different part of your system.

Click the Computer button.

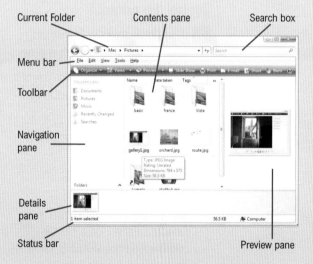

The Explorer display is highly variable. Some elements can be turned on or off, and some change in response to the material that is currently displayed. These are always present:

- The Current Folder box shows you where you are now.

- The Search box can be used to hunt for a file (see page 106).

- The Toolbar buttons vary according to what sort of folder is displayed, and what sort of

file, if any, is selected at the time.

- The Contents pane usually shows the files and folders in the current folder, though for Computer it shows the disks and other storage on the PC.

These are optional, though the first two are normally present:

- The Navigation pane has two parts: Favourite Links lets you open your most-used folders with one click; Folders shows the structure of folders – and we'll come back to this shortly.

- The Details pane tells you the size, date and other details about the selected file or folder.

- The Preview pane shows a small version of an image or the first page of other documents, if a preview is available.

- The Search pane opens up when you run an advanced search (see page 107).

- The Menu bar gives another way to reach the commands and options. Compared to the selected and context-sensitive Toolbar, which changes as you work, this has the advantage that every command is always there, and in the same place.

You will see later (page 82) how to turn these elements on and off.

The Toolbar contents vary, depending upon the file selected. These buttons are always or often there:

Organize ▾ — Shows a menu of commands for managing files

Views ▾ — Gives you different ways to look at what's in your system.

Edit ▾ — Opens a file for editing.

Print — Prints one copy of the selected file.

E-mail — Opens your email system and attaches the file to a message, ready to send to someone.

Open ▾ — Opens the selected file for reading or editing.

Share — Controls who can have access to the file.

Burn — Copies the selected file(s) to a CD or DVD.

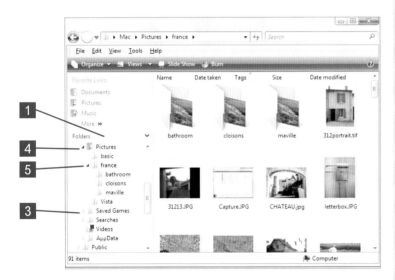

View the folders

1 If the Folders bar is closed and lying at the bottom of the Navigation pane, click on it to open it up.

2 In the Folders list, ▷ to the left shows that a drive or folder contains a lower level of folders.

3 Click ▷ to bring the next level of folders into view. The icon changes to ◢ .

4 Click ◢ when you want to hide the lower levels of folders again.

5 Click on a folder name to select it and to list its files and folders in the main part of the display.

Using Paint

There are essentially two ways to draw an image on a computer. In applications like Microsoft Draw (supplied with Word and other Office programs), the picture is made up of lines, circles, text notes, etc. each of which remains separate, and can be moved, deleted, recoloured or resized at any point.

Paint is the graphics software that comes with Windows. It uses the alternative approach. Here the image is produced by applying colour to a background, with each new line overwriting anything that may be beneath. Using this type of graphics software is very like real painting. You can wipe out a mistake while the paint is still wet, but as soon as it has dried it is fixed on the canvas – though Paint allows you to undo the last move.

Start Paint

1 Click (icon) to open the Start menu.

2 Point to All Programs to open the list of programs. Open the Accessories folder.

3 In the Accessories menu, click on Paint.

See also

You can find out about Microsoft Draw in Chapter 6.

Important

Remember that you've got to use it if you want to learn it! Run Paint and practice the techniques that are covered in these next few pages. You can easily rub out your mistakes, or if it is a real mess, start again from scratch. (Open the File menu and select New to restart.)

Paint can easily be used to produce simple diagrams, or to edit images captured from the screen.

Use the Text toolbar to format text – turn it on via the View menu.

The Toolbox

There is a simple but adequate set of tools. A little experimentation will show how they all work. Play with them! Release your inner Picasso! The notes here and on the next page may help.

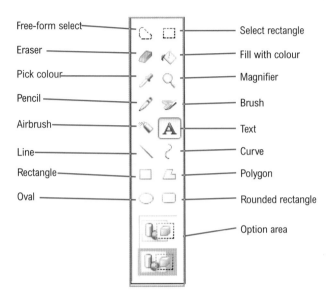

The options depend upon the tool:

- Free-form/rectangle select and Text – transparent or opaque background
- Eraser and Airbrush – size
- Magnifier – level 2×, 6× or 8×
- Brush – size and shape
- Line and curve – thickness
- Rectangle, Polygon and Oval – outline or fill only, or both.

To use the Erase, Pencil, Brush or Airbrush: click to leave a dot or blob; drag to create a line.

To draw a line: click where the line is to start and drag the end into position – you can move the line as long as you keep the button held down.

To draw a rectangle or oval: click at one corner of where the shape is to go and drag to the opposite corner. The shape will be drawn in the current line thickness – switch to the Line tool first if you want to change this.

Did you know? ?

If you hold down [Shift] when drawing, it makes ovals into circles; rectangles into squares and only allows lines to be drawn at 0°, 45° and 90°.

Drawing a curve

The curved line tool is a bit trickier than the rest. Even when you have the hang of how this works, it will still take you several goes to get a line right!

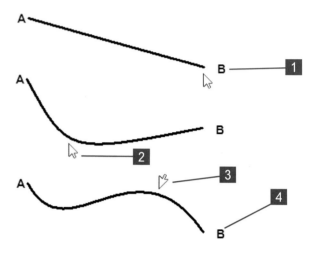

1 Draw a line between the points where the curve will start and end.

2 Click or drag to create the first curve – exaggerate the curve as it will be reduced at the next stage.

3 Drag out the second curve now – as long as the mouse button is down, the line will flex to follow the cursor.

or

4 For a single curve, just click at the end of the line.

Timesaver tip

Press [Prt Sc] to copy the whole screen to the Clipboard, or [Alt] + [Prt Sc] to copy the active window. The image can be pasted into Paint and saved. That's how the screenshots were produced for this book.

The colour palette is used in almost the same way in all Windows programs. You can select a colour from the palette – use the left button for the foreground colour and the right button for the background – or mix your own. Remember that you are mixing light, not paint. This means:

- red and green make yellow
- green and blue make cyan
- blue and red make magenta
- red, green and blue make white.

The more light you use, the lighter the colour.

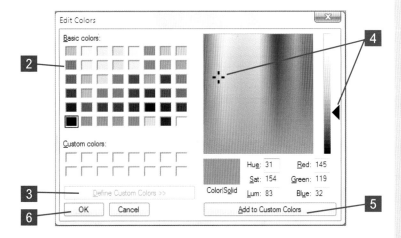

Did you know?

If you hold down the right mouse button, lines are drawn in the background colour instead of the foreground colour.

If you hold the button down while using the eraser, it replaces any current foreground colour with background colour.

1 Double-click on a colour in the palette or use Colours, Edit Colours.

2 At the Edit Colours dialogue box, click on a Basic or Custom Colour and go to Step 6.

or

3 Click [Define Custom Colors >>] to open the full box.

4 Drag the cross-hair cursor in the main square to set the Red/Green/Blue balance, and move the arrow up or down the scale to set the light/dark level.

5 Click [Add to Custom Colors] if you want to add this to the set.

6 Click [OK] – the new colour will replace the one currently selected in the palette on the main screen.

Saving an image

If you want to keep your image, or use it in another application, you need to save it as a file. The process is very similar to saving a document in WordPad.

To save a new file

1 Open the File menu and select Save As…

2 Type in a File name to identify the file clearly.

3 Click [Save].

The file will probably be saved in the Pictures folder. We will look at how to select a different folder in Chapter 3.

To resave a file

4 Open the File menu and select Save.

Did you know?

Paint can save images in half a dozen different file formats, but the default .jpg (JPEG) does the job very nicely for our purposes just now. There's more on graphic file formats in Chapter 6.

Word processors can handle other things as well as text. Even WordPad, which is probably the simplest word processor around, can cope with images. Try it now. Insert the image that you just created into your text file.

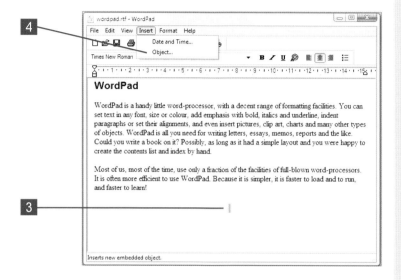

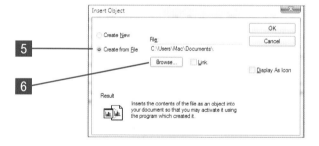

Insert an image

1 Run WordPad if it is not already open (see page 5).

2 Open the file you created earlier.

3 Click into the document at the point where you want to place the image.

4 Open the Insert menu and select Object.

5 Click Create from File.

6 Click Browse... .

Inserting an image into a document (cont.)

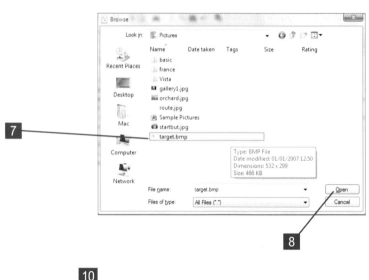

7 Select the image file.

8 Click Open.

9 The image may well not be the right size. You can change the size by dragging on the 'handles' – the little black squares – on the corners or mid-sides.

10 Save the file if you want to keep this copy with its image.

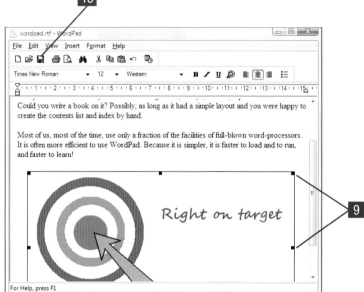

Important !

You can use the alignment buttons to change the position of an image across the width of the page. Click on the image to select it, then click the Left, Centre or Right button to set the alignment.

When you have finished work on your computer, you must shut it down properly, and not just turn it off. During a working session, application programs and Windows Vista may have created temporary files, and any data files that you have been editing may still be open in memory and not yet written safely to disk. A proper shut down closes and stores open files and removes unwanted ones.

1 Click the Start button, point to the arrow on the bottom right of the menu and select Shut Down. If any windows are open, they will be closed, and you may be prompted to save documents.

or

2 Hold down [Alt] and press [F4]. If any windows are open, this will close the topmost one. Repeat to close all open windows, then press [Alt] + [F4] again to shut down.

3 The Shut Down Windows dialogue box will appear, click on the drop-down button in the centre to open a list of alternative endings. Select one and click OK.

Shutting down (cont.)

Other endings

If you share the PC with other people, or want to stop work for a short while, there are four options on the Shut Down menu which can end a session temporarily.

- Switch User suspends your programs, and allows another user to log in. The documents that you were working on will not be affected by anything they do. When they are finished you can log in again and pick up where you left off.

- Log Off ends the programs that you have been using, but leaves the PC running, for another person to use. This is the best choice if you have finished with the PC for some time, but others will want it.

- Lock suspends your programs and switches to the blue-green Vista screen. To restart the session, you must type in your password (and there's no point in using Lock if you haven't got one). This does not tie up the PC – there is a Switch User option which will allow someone else to use it – but it does protect your work from prying eyes or careless fingers while you are away from your desk.

  You can also Lock the PC with the ⬛ button.

- Sleep shuts down the screen and hard drive, but leaves the memory active. While suspended, the power consumption is very low, but the PC can be restarted almost instantly. This is a good alternative to a full shut down if you intend to restart in less than an hour or so. Even in Sleep mode, a PC does use some power – the transformer is still active when everything else has stopped – but turning on and off frequently can accelerate wear on the circuits.

  The ⬛ button will also put the PC to sleep.

Windows essentials

2

Introduction

Windows Vista is an operating system – and more. An operating system handles the low-level interaction between the processor and the screen, memory, mouse, disk drives, printer and other peripherals. Windows Vista has drivers (control programs) for all PC-compatible processors and virtually all of the many PC peripherals on the market. The operating system is a bridge between the hardware of the computer and its applications – such as word processors and spreadsheets. As a result, whoever manufactured your PC and whatever type it is, as long as it can run the Windows Vista operating system, it can run any Windows Vista application. (It will also be able to run applications written for earlier versions of Windows.)

Although the operating system is the most important part of Windows, most of it is invisible. The visible part is the screen or Desktop. Windows is a graphical system. It uses icons (small images) to represent programs and files, and visual displays to show what is happening inside your PC. Many of the routine jobs are done by clicking on, dragging or otherwise manipulating these images, using the mouse or keyboard.

Windows is multi-tasking – it can run any number of programs at once. Each program runs in a separate area of the screen – a window – and these can be resized, moved, minimised or overlapped however you like. In practice, only a few will normally be active at the same time but that is more a reflection of the human inability to do several jobs simultaneously! A typical example of multi-tasking would be one program downloading material from the internet and another printing a long report, while you wrote a letter in a third.

This chapter covers the basic skills and concepts of working with Windows. You will learn how to use the mouse and the keyboard to select from menus, make choices, run programs and control the window layouts. You will also find out how to get help and how to cope when things go wrong.

Exploring the Desktop

Windows is a Graphical User Interface (or GUI, pronounced gooey). What this means is that you work mainly by using the mouse to point at and click on symbols on the screen, rather than by typing commands. It is largely intuitive – i.e. the obvious thing to do is probably the right thing – and it is tolerant of mistakes. Many can be corrected as long as you tackle them straight away, and many others can be corrected easily, even after time has passed.

One of the key ideas behind the design of Windows is that you should treat the screen as you would a desk, which is why Windows refers to the screen as the desktop. This is where you lay out your papers, books and tools, and you can arrange them to suit your own way of working. You may want to have more than one set of papers on the desktop at a time – so Windows lets you run several programs at once. You may want to have all your papers visible, for comparing or transferring data; you may want to concentrate on one, but have the others to hand. These – and other arrangements – are all possible.

Each program runs in its own window, and these can be arranged side by side, overlapping, or with the one you are working on filling the desktop and the others tucked out of the way, but still instantly accessible.

Just as there are many ways of arranging your desktop, so there are many ways of working with it – in fact, you are sometimes spoilt for choice!

It's your desktop. How you arrange it, and how you use it is up to you. This book will show you the simplest ways to use Windows Vista effectively.

- What you see on screen when you start Windows depends upon your Desktop settings and the shortcuts – the icons that you can click on to start programs – you are using.
- What the screen looks like once you are into your working session, is infinitely variable.
- Certain principles always apply and certain things are always there. It is the fact that all Windows applications share a common approach that makes Windows so easy to use.

Exploring the
Desktop (cont.)

Shortcuts   Menu bar   Program windows   Desktop   Gadgets

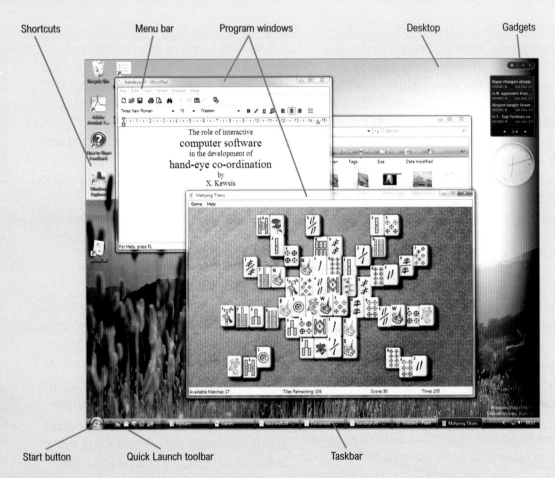

Start button   Quick Launch toolbar   Taskbar

Shortcuts – instant access to programs. You can create your own shortcuts.

Menu bar – gives access to a program's commands.

Program windows – adjust their size and placing to suit yourself.

Desktop – you can change the background picture or pattern and its colours.

Start button – you should be able to start any program on your PC from its menu.

Quick Launch toolbar – a quick way to start key programs.

Taskbar – when a program is running, it has a button here. Click on a button to open its window and bring it to the front of the desktop.

Gadgets – small programs, including a clock and various utilities that can draw information off the Internet.

Most Windows Vista operations can be handled quite happily by the mouse alone, leaving the keyboard for data entry. However, keys are necessary for some jobs, and if you prefer typing to mousing, it is possible to do most jobs from the keyboard. The relevant ones are shown here.

The function keys

Some operations can be run from these – for instance, [F1] starts up the Help system in any Windows application.

The control sets

The Arrow keys can often be used instead of the mouse for moving the cursor. Above them are more movement keys, which will let you jump around in text. [Insert] and [Delete] are also here.

Key guide

[Esc] – to escape from trouble. Use it to cancel bad choices.

[Tab] – move between objects on screen.

[Caps Lock] – only put this on when you want to type a lot of capitals. The Caps Lock light shows if it is on.

[Shift] – use it for capitals and the symbols on the number keys.

[Ctrl] or [Control] – used with other keys to give keystroke alternatives to mouse commands.

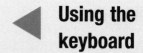 – same as clicking on the screen.

[Alt] – used, like [Ctrl], with other keys.

[Backspace] – rubs out the character to the left of the text cursor.

[Enter] – used at the end of a piece of text or to start an operation.

[Delete] – deletes files, folders and screen objects. Use with care.

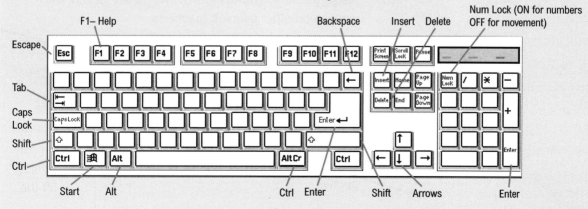

Controlling the mouse

You can't do much in Windows until you have tamed the mouse. It is used for locating the cursor, for selecting from menus, highlighting, moving and changing the size of objects, and much more. It won't bite, but it will wriggle until you have shown it who is in charge.

The mouse and the cursor

There are two main types of mice.

One type has a ball beneath. Moving the mouse rolls the ball inside it. The ball turns the sensor rollers and these transmit the movement to the cursor. To control this type of mouse effectively you need a mouse mat or a thin pad of paper – it won't run well on a hard surface.

The other type uses infrared to scan the area beneath and work out which way the mouse has moved. This type needs some kind of image or pattern beneath it – it won't know where it is on a plain surface.

With either type:

- If you reach the edge of the mat or whatever you are using as a mouse run, so that you cannot move the cursor any further, pick up the mouse and plonk it back into the middle.
- You can set up the mouse so that when the mouse is moved faster, the cursor moves further. Watch out for this when working on other people's machines.

Mouse actions

- Point – move the cursor with your fingers off the buttons.
- Click – the left button to select a file, menu item or other object.
- Right-click (click the right button) to open a menu of commands that can be applied to the object beneath the pointer.

- Double-click to run programs. You can set the gap between clicks to suit yourself.
- Drag – keep the left button down while moving the mouse. Used for resizing, drawing and similar jobs.
- Drag and drop – drag an object and release the left button when it is in the right place. Used for moving objects.

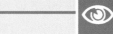

See also

Controlling the mouse, page 179, to find out how to adjust the responsiveness of the mouse to suit your hand.

2

Using the Start menu

Clicking on  at the bottom left of the screen opens the Start menu. Your menu will look a little different to mine – you can adapt the Start menu, and it will adapt to you automatically.

At the top left are links to your browser and email software (normally Internet Explorer and Windows Mail).

Beneath these are links to your most-used programs – initially this will be empty.

At the bottom left is the All Programs link.

Just above the Start button is the Search box. Use this to track down files on your computer (see page 106).

At the top right are links to Documents, Pictures and other folders where documents and files are commonly stored.

Recent Items holds a list of your lastest documents. Selecting one from this list will run the relevant application and open the file for you to work on.

You can configure your PC through the Control Panel (Chapter 7). You may have a link to the Printers, and/or a Connect To link which leads to your connections for going online.

Help and Support starts the Help system (page 41).

The three buttons on the right offer different ways to end the session (see page 21).

Jargon buster

Document – Windows uses 'document' to mean any file created by any application. A word-processed report is obviously a document, but so is a picture file from a graphics package, a data file from a spreadsheet, a video clip, sound file – in fact, any file produced by any program.

There are many situations where you have to specify a filename or an option. Sometimes you have to type in what you want, but in most cases, it only takes a click of the mouse or a couple of keystrokes.

Menus

In any Windows application, you can find all of its commands and options on the menus, with each menu containing a set of related commands. Menus drop down from the menu bar. To make one drop down, click on its name with the mouse, or press the [Alt] key and the underlined letter – usually the initial.

To select an item from a menu, click on it or type its underlined letter.

Some items are toggles. Selecting them turns an option on or off. ✔ beside the name shows that the option is on.

▶ after an item shows that another menu leads from it.

If you select an item with three dots ... after it, a dialogue box will open to get more information from you.

Dialogue boxes

These vary, but will usually have these buttons:

OK click when you have set the options, selected the file or whatever. This confirms your choices and closes the box.

Apply click to fix the options selected so far, but keep the box open for further work.

Cancel click if you decide the choices are all wrong.

to get Help on items in the box.

Click or press [Alt] + [V]

Point to open sub-menu

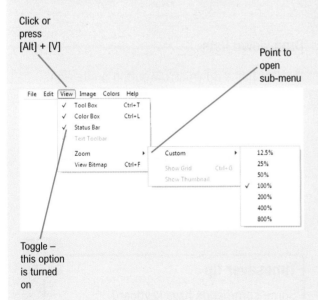

Toggle – this option is turned on

Understanding menus and dialogue boxes (cont.)

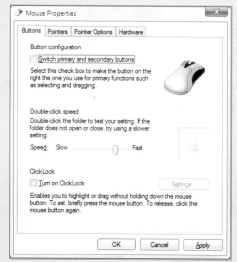

Tabs and panels

Some dialogue boxes have several sets of options in them, each on a separate panel. These are identified by tabs at the top. Click on a tab to bring its panel to the front. Usually clicking OK on any panel will close the whole box. Use Apply when you have finished with one panel but want to explore others before closing.

Check boxes

These are used where there are several options, and you can use as many as you like at the same time.

✔ in the box shows that the option has been selected.

If the box is grey and the caption faint, the option is 'greyed out' – not available at that time for the selected item.

These are selected

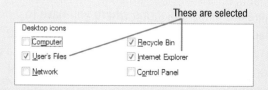

Radio buttons

These are used for either/or options. Only one of the set can be selected.

The selected option is shown by a black blob in the middle.

This one is selected

Drop-down lists

If a slot has a down arrow button on its right, click the button to drop down a list.

Click on an item in the list to select.

Click here…

Select from the list

Timesaver tip

Some commands have keyboard shortcuts. These are sometimes the [F…] keys, but often [Ctrl] + a letter. If there is a shortcut it will usually be shown on the menu after the command name.

If you click the right button on almost any object on screen in Windows Vista, a short menu will open beside it. This contains a set of commands and options that can be applied to the object.

What is on the menu depends upon the type of object and its context – hence the name. Two are shown here to give an idea of the possibilities.

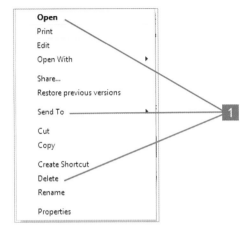

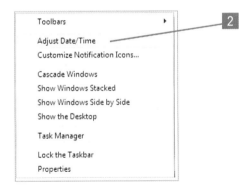

1 Files can be opened, sent to a removable disk or off in the mail, and deleted – amongst other things.

2 Adjust the clock and arrange the screen display.

Working with window frames

The frame contains all the controls you need for adjusting the display.

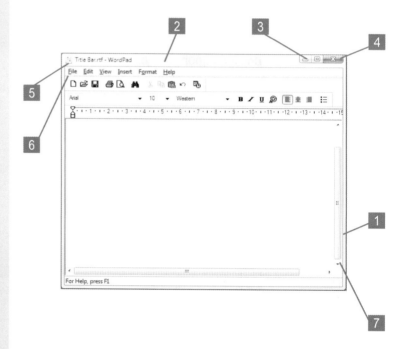

1. The frame edge has a control system built into it. When a window is in Restore mode – i.e. smaller than full-screen – you can drag on the edge to make it larger or smaller.

2. The title bar is to remind you of where you are – in the active application (the one you are using) the Close button on the bar is red. Drag on the bar to move a window.

3. The Maximise, Minimise and Restore buttons change the display mode.

4. The Close button is one of several ways to close a window and the program that was running in it.

5. The Control menu can be used for changing the screen mode or closing the window.

6. The Menu bar usually sits just below the Title bar and contains the names of its drop-down menus.

7. The Scroll bars are present on the right side and bottom of the frame if the display contained by the window is too big to fit within it.

Important

Some applications can handle several documents at once, each in its own window. These are used in almost the same way as program windows. The applications usually have a Window menu containing controls for the document windows.

What you can see in a window is often only part of the story. The working area of the application may well be much larger. If there are scroll bars on the side and/or bottom of the window, this tells you that there is more material outside the frame. The Sliders in the Scroll bars show you where your view is, relative to the overall display. Moving these allows you to view a different part of the display.

Working area

Arrow buttons

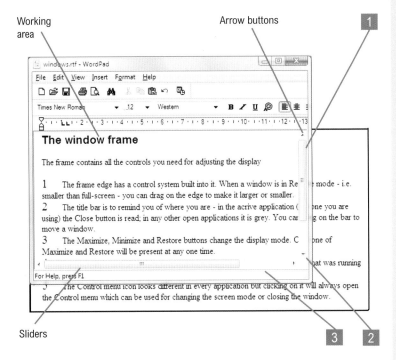

Sliders

1. Drag the slider to scroll the view in the window. Drag straight along the bar or it won't work!

2. Click an arrow button to edge the slider towards it. Hold down for a slow continuous scroll.

3. Click on the bar beside the slider to make it jump towards where you are clicking.

Changing the window mode

All programs are displayed on screen in windows, and these can normally have three modes:

- Maximised – filling the whole screen.
- Minimised – not displayed, though still present as a button on the Taskbar.
- Restore – adjustable in size and in position.

Clicking on the buttons in the top right corner of the frame is the simplest way to switch between Maximise and Restore modes, and to Minimise a window.

A window in Restore mode   A Maximised window   The current window is highlighted

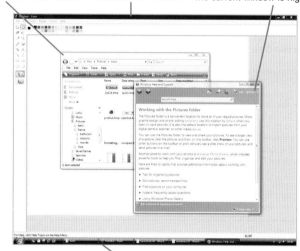

Minimised – not visible except for this.

To make a window full-screen: Click ⬜.

To shrink a window to a Taskbar button: Click ▬. To redisplay it, click on its Taskbar button.

To restore a window to variable size: Click ⧉.

Did you know?

You can change window modes using the Control menu. Click the icon at the top left of the window to open it. This menu came from a full-screen window, so Maximise is shown in grey as it does not apply. One from a variable-size window would have Restore in grey.

You can open the menu using the keys:

[Alt]+[Space] opens the Control menu of an application.

[Alt]+[–] (minus) opens the Control menu of a document.

ē	Restore	
	Move	
	Size	
–	Minimize	
◻	Maximize	
x	**Close**	Alt+F4

Timesaver tip

When you minimise a document window within an application, it shrinks to a tiny title bar, with just enough room for a name and the icons. Click Maximise or Restore to open it out again.   🔳 budg... ⬜ ◻ ✖

If you want to have two or more windows visible at the same time, you will have to arrange them on your desktop. There are Windows tools that will do it for you, or you can do it yourself.

If you right-click the Taskbar, its menu has options to arrange the windows on the desktop. Similar options are on the Window menu of most applications, to set the layout within the programs.

Cascade places the windows overlapping with only the title bars of the back ones showing.

Show Windows Stacked and Show Windows Side by Side arrange open windows side by side, or one above the other – with more than three windows, the tiling is in both directions. As the window frames take up space, the actual working area is significantly reduced. Obviously, larger, high-resolution screens are better for multi-window work, but even on a 1,280 × 1,024 display you cannot do much serious typing in a tiled window.

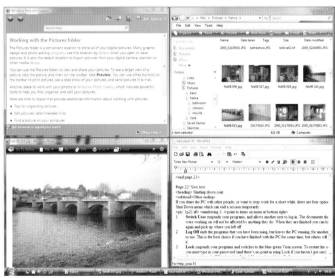

Arranging windows

1 Maximise or Restore the windows that you want to include in the layout. Minimise those that you will not be using actively.

2 Right-click the Taskbar to open its menu.

3 Select Show Windows Stacked or Show Windows Side by Side.

4 If you only want to work in one window at a time, Maximise it, and Restore it back into the arrangement when you have finished.

5 If you want to adjust the balance of the layout, you can move and resize the windows.

Important

Cascade works better than tiling on small screens.

Timesaver tip

It is generally simplest to work with the active window Maximised and any others Minimised out of the way.

Moving windows

When a window is in Restore mode – open but not full screen – it can be moved anywhere on the screen.

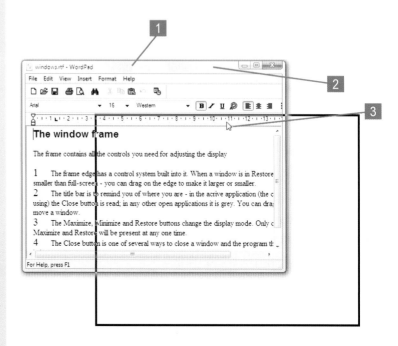

1. If the title bar isn't highlighted, click on the window to make it the active one.

2. Point at the title bar and hold the left button down.

3. Drag the window to its new position – you will only see a grey outline moving.

4. Release the button.

Important

If you are not careful it can be moved almost off the screen! Fortunately, at least a bit of the title bar will still be visible, and that is the handle you need to grab to pull it back into view.

When a window is in Restore mode, you can change its size and shape by dragging the edges of the frame to new positions. Combined with the moving facility, this lets you arrange your desktop exactly the way you like it.

1 Move the pointer to the edge or corner that you want to pull in or out.

2 When you see the double-headed arrow, hold down the left mouse button and drag the outline to the required size.

3 Release the button.

Important

The resize pointers only appear when the pointer is just on an edge, and they disappear again if you go too far. Practise! You'll soon get the knack of catching them.

Timesaver tip

You can drag any edge or corner, but the quickest way to get a window the right size, in the right place, is to use the bottom right size handle to set the shape, then drag the window into position.

Closing windows

Closing an active window

1. Click  or press [Alt]+[F4].

Closing from the Taskbar

2. Right-click the program's Taskbar button to get its menu.

3. Select Close.

4. If you have forgotten to save your work, take the opportunity that is offered to you.

When you close a window, you close down the program that was running inside it.

If you haven't saved your work, most programs will point this out and give you a chance to save before closing.

There are at least five different ways of closing. Here are the simplest three:

- If the window is in Maximised or Restore mode, click the Close icon at the top right of the Title bar. (If your mouse control is not too good, you may well do this when you are trying to Maximise the window!)

- If the window has been Minimised onto the Taskbar, right-click on its button to open the Control menu and use Close.

- If you prefer working from keys, press [Alt]+[F4].

Windows Vista has its own special Help and Support system. It's very comprehensive and has some excellent features, but – most unhelpfully – it looks and feels different from the standard application Help systems.

The main Windows Vista Help system is reached through the Help and Support item on the Start menu.

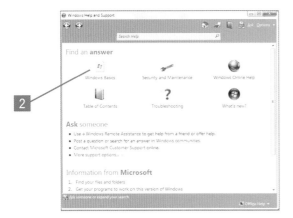

Getting Help and Support

1 Click and select Help and Support.

2 Click an icon to select a route into the Help system – choose Basics this time.

Important

You can set up your system so that it only uses the Help on your hard disk, or get it to include the online Help and Support at Microsoft. If you have an always-on broadband connection to the Internet, online is normally the best choice, because it will give you access to more and better Help. To change the setting:

1 Click the Offline Help (or Online Help) button at the bottom right of the window.

2 Select Get online/offline Help to change the setting for the current session.

or

3 Select Settings.

4 Tick (or clear) the Include Windows Online… option.

5 Click OK.

Getting Help and Support (cont.)

3 Scroll through the list and click on a topic.

4 Click on the terms in green to get an explanation of the terminology.

3

Did you know?

Text in blue is usually a link to another Help article. If the text has an arrow at the start, it tells you that clicking on it will start a program, open a dialogue box, or do something similar. The Help article will stay open, so that you can read it while you try out the program, or set options.

> **To add an e-mail account in Windows Mail**
>
> 1. → Click to open Windows Mail.

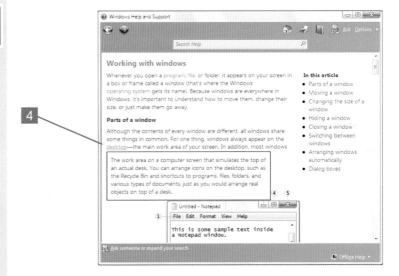

4

The Contents gives you access to the entire Help system. It is arranged into 15 main areas, which are subdivided into subtopics – each of which may be further subdivided.

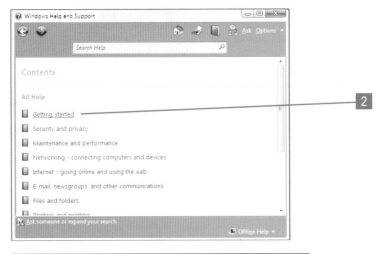

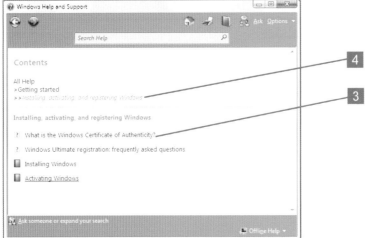

Using the Help Table of Contents

1 In the main Help and Support window, click the Table of Contents icon or its title.

2 Folder headings have a block to the left. Click on a heading to open its folder. You will see a list of articles and headings for subtopics.

3 Article headings have a question mark to the left. Click on the heading to read the article.

4 At the top of the window you will see a list of the headings that you have clicked through to reach the current place. Click on any of these to jump back to that heading.

Timesaver tip

Don't forget the troubleshooting guides. You can reach these from the main Help and Support window. They can be very useful for solving common problems, such as difficulties with printers or other peripherals, or when you are trying to configure your Internet and email software. They will normally take you through a series of checks to diagnose problems and can often tell you what to do to cure them.

Searching for Help

1 Type one or more keywords into the box and press the [Enter] key.

2 The 'best' 30 results, i.e. those which Vista calculates as best matching your search, will be listed. Click on a heading to display the page.

3 If you don't find what you want, try different keywords. Sometimes it is better not to be too specific.

The Search box is present on every page of the Help system.

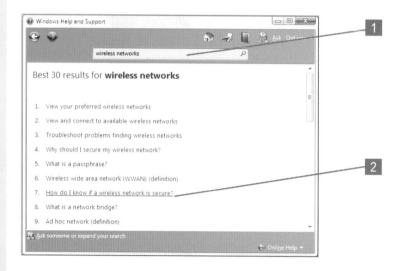

Jargon buster

Keyword – any word which might occur in the pages that you are looking for. If you give two or more, the system will only list pages which contain all those words.

Windows Vista is a pretty stable system, but things do go wrong. A 'crash' can occur at several levels.

- A program may simply misbehave – it will still run, but not respond or update the screen correctly. Close it – saving any open files – and run it again. If it still behaves badly, close down all your programs and restart the PC.
- The system will 'hang' – i.e. nothing is happening and it will not respond to the mouse or normal keyboard commands. If the [Control] + [Alt] + [Del] keystroke works, you can reach the Task Manager to close the offending application, which may get things moving again.
- You get a total lock up where it will not pick up [Control] + [Alt] + [Del]. Press the little restart button on the front of the PC. It is there for just these times!

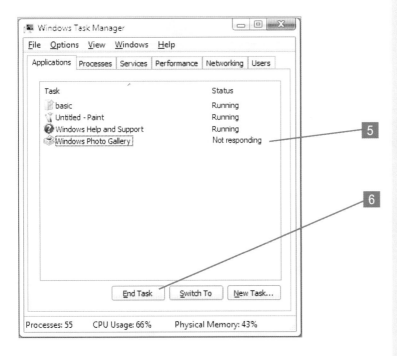

Handling crashes with the Task Manager

Misbehaving program

2

1 Open the program's File menu and select Exit (or Close) – saving files if prompted.

2 Restart the program.

Hung system

3 Press [Control] + [Alt] + [Delete] together.

4 The desktop is replaced by a blue-green screen with options for locking or logging off. The last option is Start Task Manager. Click here.

5 At the Task Manager dialogue box, select the one marked 'not responding'.

6 Click End Task .

7 Restart the program.

Dead keyboard

8 Press the Restart button on the front of the PC.

Simple word processing

Introduction

Word processing is probably the most widely used computer application, and the most widely used word processing software is Microsoft Word. You probably have Word on your machine. It is often included in 'package deals' on new PCs, and supplied ready-installed – if yours is new, and you are still exploring it, have a look for Word now. Is it on the Programs group on the Start menu? If you cannot see a 'Microsoft Word' item on the main list, is there a 'Microsoft Office' sub-menu containing Word? Word is also included in some versions of the Works software suite, which is also commonly bundled with new PCs.

If you do not have Word on your PC, don't go out and buy it unless you really need its advanced facilities, as Windows comes with a perfectly good, if slightly limited, word processor. WordPad can handle letters, reports, minutes of meetings, simple brochures and newsletters, and has much the same formatting facilities as Word. It is, in effect, a cut-down version of Word, with the same commands and toolbar buttons – but just not as many of them. In this chapter, the examples and instructions are for Word, but virtually all of them apply equally well to WordPad.

What you'll do

Explore the Word screen

Start a new document

Select text

Edit text

Undo mistakes

Emphasise text

Set fonts

Change the text size

Use the Font dialogue box

Colour your text

Align text

Set the line spacing

Define the Page Setup

Save a document

Print a document

Use Print Preview

Get Help

Find Help through the Contents

Exploring the Word screen

The main part of the screen forms the working area, where you type your text and insert graphics and other objects to create your documents. Around this area are:

- The Title bar, showing the name of the document, and carrying the usual Minimise, Maximise/Restore and Close application buttons.
- The Menu bar, giving you access to all of Word's many features.
- The toolbars – normally only the Standard and Formatting toolbars are open, but others can be displayed as required. The toolbars are usually on the top and side of the working area, but can be moved or floated.
- The scroll bars, used for moving around your document – just drag the sliders or click the arrows at the ends to scroll the display. At the bottom of the right scroll bar are buttons for

moving between pages; and at the left of the bottom bar are four buttons for changing the view. Click on each of these to see the effect – Normal or Print Layout views are best for most work.

- The ruler, showing the margins, indents and tabs. This is not present in some views.
- The Status bar, showing where you are in the document, what language the spell checker is using, and the state of various toggle (on/off) options.

The area on the right of the window is sometimes occupied by the Task pane. When you first run Word, there will be a range of options here for starting new files or opening existing ones. The Task pane is also used for inserting clip art, formatting, the Clipboard and other functions. It can be closed when not needed.

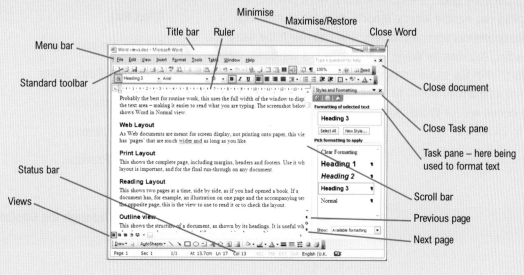

Word views

Word offers you five ways to look at a document.

Normal view

Probably the best view for routine work, this uses the full width of the window to display the text area – making it easier to read what you are typing. The screenshot below shows Word in Normal view.

Web Layout view

As Web documents are meant for screen display, not printing onto paper, this view has 'pages' that are much wider and as long as you like.

Print Layout view

This shows the complete page, including margins, headers and footers. Use it when layout is very important, and for the final run-through on any document.

Reading Layout view

This is designed for reading and marking up an existing document. To create more viewing areas, all the toolbars are removed except the Reading and Reviewing ones. Pages can be viewed one or two at a time.

Outline view

This shows the structure of a document, as shown by its headings. It is useful when planning a new document, and simplifies reorganising long, multi-page ones.

3

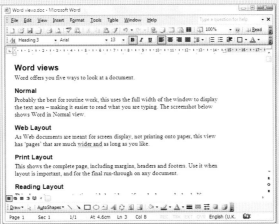

Normal view

Exploring the Word screen (cont.)

Changing views

1 To switch between views, use the buttons at the bottom left of the screen.

or

2 Open the View menu.

3 Select a view.

Print Layout view

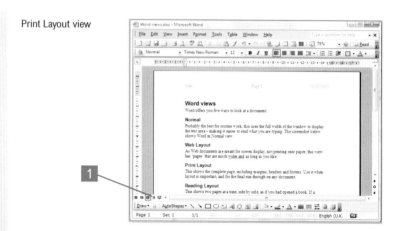

Reading Layout view

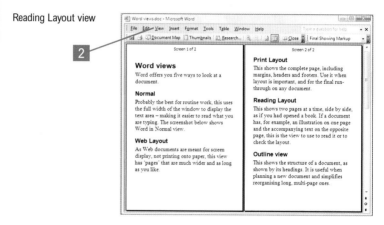

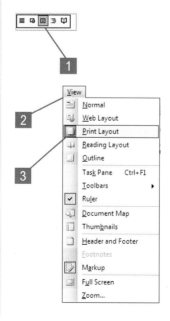

All documents start from some kind of template which sets up the basic design. That bare white page that you see when you first start Word is in fact a 'blank document' template. In this case it simply sets the page size and the fonts for the normal and heading text. Other templates may have some text or images already in place – headed paper for letters, for example – and/or have more elaborate design features or suggestions for content and layout of the items to include in the new document.

Starting a new document

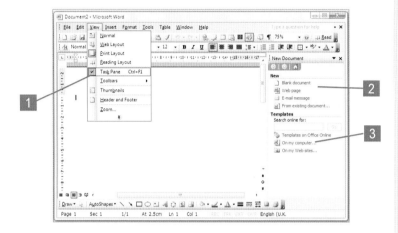

Explore the templates

1 If the Task pane is not visible, open it from the View menu.

2 Select Blank Document or Web Page.

or

3 In the Templates section select On my computer …

4 At the Templates dialogue box, select a tab.

5 Click on a template to see its preview.

6 When you find a suitable template, click [OK].

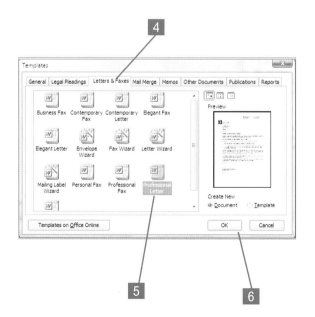

Timesaver tip

If you just want to start a new blank document, click the New button.

Starting a new document (cont.)

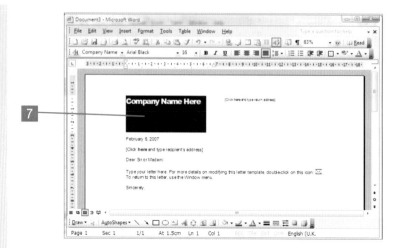

7 Click into the prompts and replace them with your own details.

Important

Word has two typing modes: Insert and Overtype. In Insert mode, when you type into existing text the new characters push the old ones along to make room. In Overtype mode new text replaces the old. (The OVR indicator on the Status line is in bold when you are in Overtype mode.) Press the [Insert] key to switch between them.

When you start typing on a blank page, the text will first appear at the top left corner and gradually fill down. In an existing document, text is placed at the insertion point – the flashing line. If this is not where you want to type, click to move the insertion point to the right place.

Before you can do any kind of editing, you must first select the text. A block of text can be any size, from one character to the whole document. How you select depends upon the size of block that you want.

Click here to select the line   You can start to select at any point

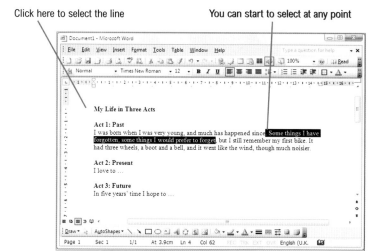

To select:

■ A word – double-click anywhere in the word.

■ A line – click in the margin to the left of the line.

■ A paragraph – triple-click inside the paragraph.

■ Any other text – click at the start of the block and drag to the end.

■ Any size block – move the insertion point to the start of the block, hold down [Shift] and move to the end using keystrokes.

3

Selecting text (cont.)

Using keys in Word

If you make a mistake, use [Backspace] to erase the character(s) that you have just typed.

If you spot a mistake later, click the insertion point into the text and use [Backspace] to erase to its left or [Delete] to erase to its right, or select the text and press [Delete].

To move around the text using the keys:

- [Arrows] – one character left or right, one line up or down; one word left or right if [Ctrl] is held down.

- [PgUp] – move one screenful up.

- [PgDn] – move one screenful down.

- [Home] – jump to the start of the line; or the start of the text if [Ctrl] is held down.

- [End] – jump to the end of the line; or the end of the text if [Ctrl] is held down.

Timesaver tip

If you want to select all the text in a document, press [Ctrl] and [A].

Important

In Word the cursor is an I-beam, rather than an arrow pointer. This is to help you position it more accurately in the text.

When word processing, you should never have to type anything twice. If you need to use the same words several times, text can be copied. If text is in the wrong place, it can be moved.

There are two main techniques for copying and moving text.

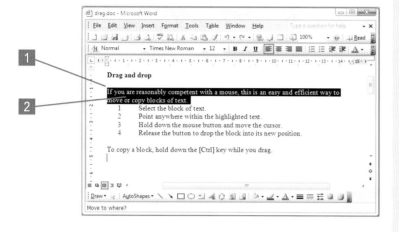

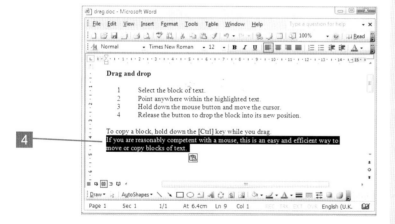

Drag and drop

If you are reasonably competent with a mouse, this is an easy and efficient way to move or copy blocks of text.

1 Select the block of text.

2 Point anywhere within the highlighted text.

3 Hold down the mouse button and move the cursor (now ⛶).

4 Release the button to drop the block into its new position.

To copy a block, hold down the [Ctrl] key while you drag.

3

Editing text (cont.)

Cut, Copy and Paste

1 Select the block of text.

2 Click 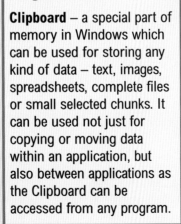.

or

3 Open the Edit menu or right-click and select Cut or Copy.

4 Place the cursor where you want the text.

5 Click 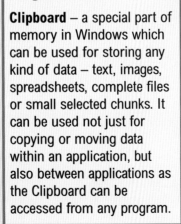.

or

6 Open the Edit menu or right-click and select Paste.

The Edit menu of every Windows application has the commands Cut, Copy and Paste. You will also find them on the context menu that opens when you right-click on an object, and there are buttons for them on the Standard toolbar. These are used for copying and moving data within and between applications.

Cut deletes a selected block of text, picture, file or other object, but places a copy in the Clipboard.

Copy copies the selected data into the Clipboard.

Paste copies the data from the Clipboard into a different place in the same application, or into a different application – as long as this can handle data in that format.

The data remains in the Clipboard until new data is copied into it, or until Windows is shut down.

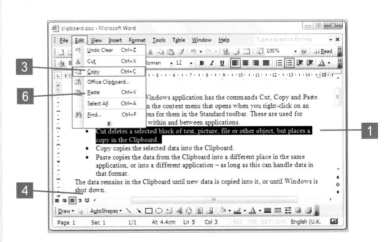

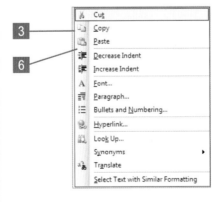

The Cut operation is the same as Copy except that it deletes the selected block of text, picture, file or whatever object, when it places a copy in the Clipboard.

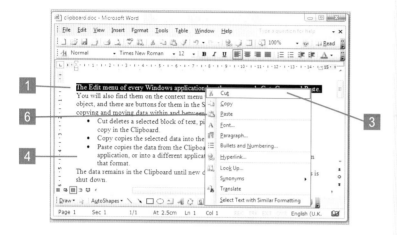

To move text

1 Select the block of text.

2 Click [✂].

or

3 Open the Edit menu or right-click and select Cut.

4 Place the cursor where you want the text.

5 Click [📋].

or

6 Open the Edit menu or right-click and select Paste.

Timesaver tip

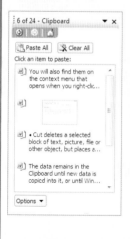

Word, like the other programs in the Microsoft Office suite, has its own Clipboard. It can hold 24 items and is controlled through the Task pane. If the Clipboard does not open automatically, use Edit, Office Clipboard to open it. In the Clipboard, you can select an item to paste or click Paste All to copy all the items at once. The standard Edit, Paste pastes in the last item cut or copied, as normal.

Undoing mistakes

In the old days, you were lucky if your software allowed you to undo a mistake. With Word, you can go back and undo a whole series of actions. This doesn't just protect you from your mistakes, it also gives you freedom to experiment. You can do major editing or reformatting, and if at the end you preferred things how they were, you can undo your way back to it. This is managed through the Undo button.

To undo one action

1 Click the arrow on the Undo button.

To undo a series of actions

2 Open the list from the Undo button.

3 Point down the list to highlight all the actions that you want to undo.

4 Click the left mouse button.

Redo

This is the undo-undo button! If you undid too much, use this to put it back again.

Use it for the last action, or a whole sequence, exactly as with Undo.

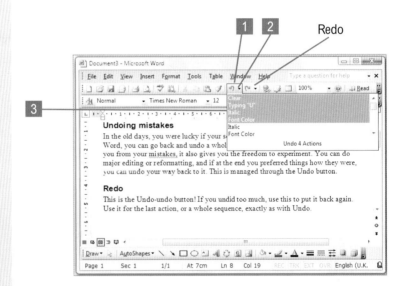

Redo

You can add emphasis to text in several ways. The simplest is to make it **bold**, *italic* or <u>underlined</u>.

These options can be used by themselves, or in combination – this is ***bold and italic*** – to pick out words within a paragraph, to emphasise whole paragraphs or to make headings stand out more.

You can set these options using the buttons on the Formatting toolbar, the Font dialogue box or the keystroke shortcuts.

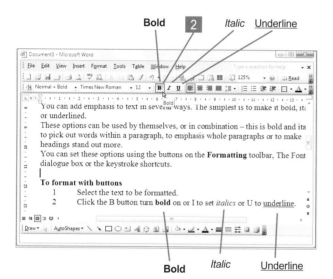

Bold   2   *Italic*   <u>Underline</u>

Bold   *Italic*   <u>Underline</u>

Emphasising text

To format with buttons

1 Select the text to be formatted.

2 Click the **B** button to turn Bold on or *I* to set italics or <u>U</u> to <u>underline</u>.

To remove the formatting

3 Select the text again and click the same button to turn the effect off.

3

Timesaver tip

You can format text with these keystroke shortcuts:

Press [Control] and [B] to set Bold

Press [Control] and [I] to set Italic

Press [Control] and [U] to set Underline.

Setting fonts

A font is a typeface design, identified by name. There are many thousands of fonts around – Windows comes equipped with several dozen.

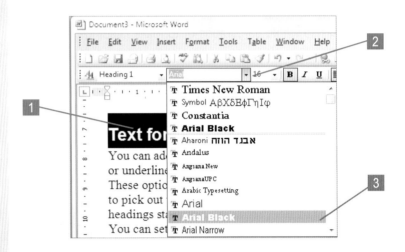

To set the font

1 Select the text to be formatted.

2 Click the ⊡ button to the right of the font name to drop down the list – the names are set in their own fonts, so you have examples.

3 Select an option from the list.

Did you know?

Fonts can be grouped into four overall categories.

Serif fonts have little 'tails' (the serifs) on the end the long strokes. They are usually very 'readable' and so are normally used for large amounts of text. Popular serif fonts include Times New Roman, Georgia and Garamond.

T T

Serif   Sans

Sans serif fonts have simpler lines. They are often used for headings, captions, children's books and other places where small amounts of clear text are wanted. This is Arial. Other sans serif fonts include Helvetica and Tahoma.

Display fonts are those where the visual effect is more important than readability. They are mainly used for headings and in advertisements or posters, where maximum impact is needed. Some display fonts are: **Impact**, Remedy, *Calligraphy* and **STENCIL** .

Picture fonts are sets of special characters and images which can be 'typed' into text. They are mainly used for formulae, marking bullet lists or other special effects. Examples include $\alpha\beta\chi$©$\sum$ (Symbol) and ☎☺☻❶❷➜ (Wingdings).

The size of the text can be set from the drop-down list beside the Font on the Formatting toolbar.

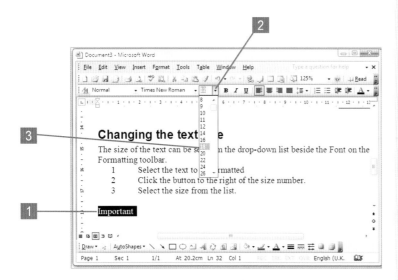

1. Select the text to be formatted.
2. Click the ⊡ button to the right of the size number.
3. Select the size from the list.

Important !

It is usually best to set the font before the size as some fonts are larger than others with the same nominal size. You should see how big the characters look before you set the size.

3

Using the Font dialogue box

If you want to set several font options at the same time – perhaps to make a heading larger, bold and in a different font – or you want to set one of the less-used options, you can use the Font dialogue box.

1 Select the text to be formatted.

2 Open the Format menu and select Font…

3 At the Font dialogue box, make sure that you are on the Font tab.

4 Set the font, style, size and/or other options as required.

5 Check the Preview and adjust the settings if necessary.

6 Click OK.

Did you know?

Text size is normally measured in points. This text is 12 point. It can be any size, though you do not usually see it under 6 point or over 72 point in books or magazines.

6 point

9 point

12 point

24 point

48 point

Word offers you two ways to colour text. You can set the font colour – the ink, as it were – or highlight the text by colouring the 'paper' behind it. There are two differences between using text colour and using highlights:

- With highlights you have a smaller choice of colours.
- The Highlight tool can be turned on so that you go through a piece highlighting lots of different words and phrases without having to reselect the tool every time.

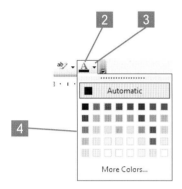

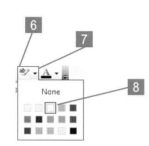

To turn on the highlighter

Do not select text, if any is selected already, deselect it by clicking once anywhere on the document.

Open the Highlight palette and pick a colour. The cursor will now have a little highlighter icon next to the I beam. Drag the highlighter over the text to be coloured. Repeat as required.

To return to normal editing, click once on the Highlight button.

Colouring your text

To set the Font colour

1. Select the text.
2. Click the Font colour button to apply the current colour.

   or

3. Click ⊡ beside the Font colour button.
4. Pick a colour from the palette.

To highlight text

5. Select the text.
6. Click the Highlight button to apply the current highlight colour.

   or

7. Click ⊡ beside the Highlight button.
8. Pick a colour from the palette.

3

Aligning text

The alignment settings control the position of text in relation to the margins.

The alignment options can only be applied to whole paragraphs. A paragraph is selected if any part of it is selected or it contains the insertion point.

In Word, the simplest way to set alignment is to use the toolbar buttons.

Left aligned text is flush with the left margin, but ragged on the right-hand side. It is the default in Word. This text is left aligned.

> Right aligned text is flush with the right margin. A common example of its use is for the sender's address on a letter.

Centre alignment sets each line mid-way between the margins. Headings are often centred.

Justified text makes the words flush with the margins on both sides. It gives a page a neater look than left alignment, but can sometimes produce wide gaps between words.

1 Select the paragraph(s) to be formatted. To select a single paragraph, click anywhere inside it. To select several paragraphs in a block, click anywhere inside the first, then drag the highlight down to anywhere in the last.

2 Click the appropriate toolbar button.

Left   **2**   Centre   Right   Justified

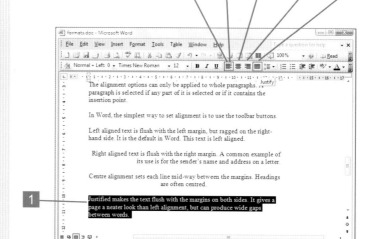

Timesaver tip

You can also use these keystroke shortcuts:

Press [Control] and [L] for Left alignment

Press [Control] and [R] for Right alignment

Press [Control] and [E] for Centre alignment

Press [Control] and [J] for Justified.

Line spacing refers to the amount of vertical space between lines of text. The spacing can only be applied to whole paragraphs and is probably best set through the Paragraph dialogue box.

Text is normally set with single line spacing, so that there is a slim gap between the bottom of one line and the top of the next. This paragraph has single line spacing.

Double spacing is typically used where people want to leave room

between the lines for handwritten notes on the printed copy.

The line spacing can also be set to 1.5 lines or specified in

points, a measure used by printers and publishers.

1 Select the paragraph(s).

2 Open the Format menu and select Paragraph…

3 Switch to the Indents and Spacing tab if it is not already on top.

4 Drop down the Line spacing list and select the level.

3

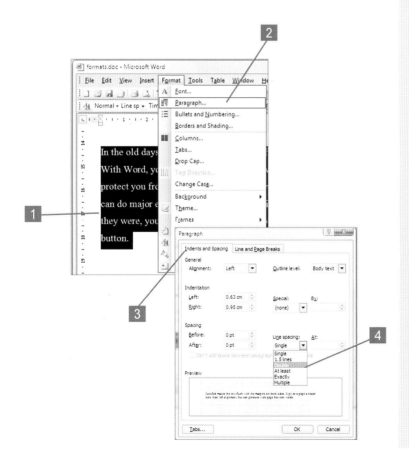

Defining the Page Setup

1. Open the File menu and select Page Setup.

2. On the Margins tab, use the buttons to adjust the margins or enter new values.

3. Set the Orientation – Portrait or Landscape.

4. If required, turn on Mirror margins or 2 pages per sheet.

5. On the Paper tab, pick the Paper size.

6. On the Layout tab, set the Section start and Header and Footer options for large or multi-section documents, if appropriate.

7. Click OK.

If you are creating anything other than routine letters and memos, the Page Setup may well need changing.

Paper size

You will need to change the size if you are printing on envelopes or unusual paper, and should always check it when working from a template, which may have been set up for US paper size. Use this tab also to set the orientation – upright (Portrait) or sideways (Landscape).

Setting margins

Use the Margins tab to adjust the space around the printed area. Margins should not be too small – printers can't reach the very edge of the paper and you need some white space around any text. Sometimes a slight reduction of the margins will give you a better printout. There is little more irritating than a couple of odd lines of text or a tiny block of data on a separate sheet.

If you are printing both sides of the paper, book-style, tick the Mirror margins box. If they are to be ring-bound, widen the inner margin or set the gutter (the space inside the inner margin) to allow for the hidden paper.

Paper source

This rarely needs attention. You might perhaps want to turn off the defaults so that you can manually feed in individual sheets of card or special paper, without emptying the paper tray.

Layout

This needs attention with large documents that have been divided into sections – you can set where each section starts – and where you have headers and footers, and don't want the same ones on every page.

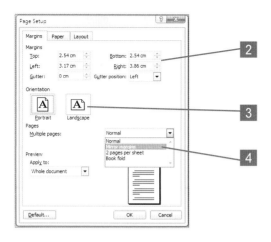

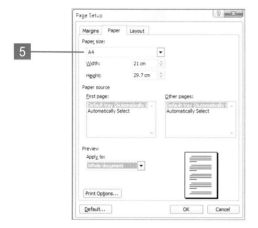

Did you know?

With mirror margins, the margins are Inside/Outside not Left/Right.

3

Saving a document

There are two file-saving routines in Word, as in most Windows applications.

- Save is used to save an existing file after editing – just click or open the File menu and select Save.
- Save As is used to save a new file, or to save an existing file with a new name or in a new folder – see the steps.

1 Click to save a new file.

or

2 Open the File menu and select Save As to save a file with a new name or location.

3 Set the Save in folder.

4 Enter the Filename.

5 Change the Save as type setting if required.

6 Click Save.

7 Return to editing, or exit, as desired.

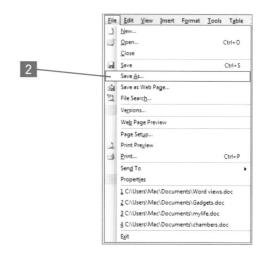

Timesaver tip

You can save in different formats if you need to transfer documents to other applications.

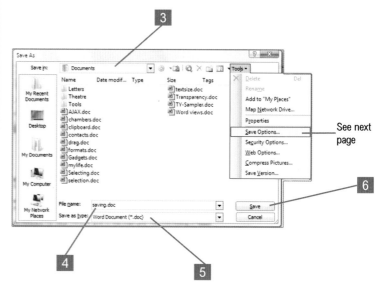

See next page

Save options

If you select General Options from the Tools drop-down list on the Save dialogue box, it opens an extensive Options panel in Word. The key options are those which protect the file:

- Password to open, prevents all unauthorised access.
- Password to modify allows anyone to read it, but only the password holder can save it, with the same name.
- Read recommended sets Read Only as the default mode for opening the file.
- If you have any doubts about the PC's reliability, turn on Always create Backup copy.
- Save AutoRecover guards against lost work – you should set a reasonable interval.

If you have any doubts about the PC's reliability, turn on Always create Backup copy

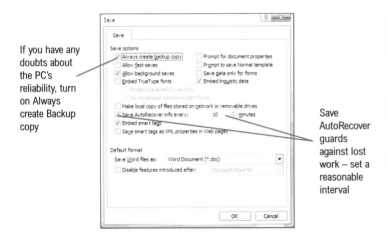

Save AutoRecover guards against lost work – set a reasonable interval

Printing a document

Word is WYSIWYG (What You See Is What You Get), so that what you see on screen is very close to its appearance when printed. Because of this, using the Print button on the Standard toolbar works well most of the time. If you want to print selected pages, or need several copies, or have other special requirements, the Print dialogue box gives you more control of the output.

To control the printing

1. If you only want to print part of a page, select the text first.

2. Open the File menu and select Print.

3. Set the range of pages to print.

4. Set the Copies number – turn on Collate to print multiple copies in sorted sets.

5. For double-sided printing, set the Print option to Odd pages, then feed the paper back in – in reverse order – and repeat with Even pages.

6. Click OK.

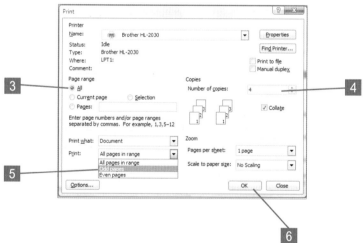

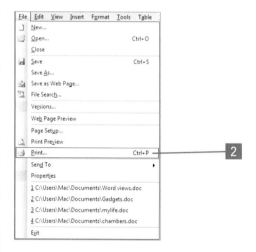

Timesaver tip

To print one copy of the whole document, using the default printer, just click .

If you work in Print Layout view, you can see – as you create the document – how it will fit on paper. By dropping the Zoom level down to Whole page or Two pages, you can get a better impression of the overall layout of the document.

Print Preview lets you view more pages – as thumbnails – at a time, has a Zoom tool which you can use to jump between 100% and the preview size, and shows the headers and footers more clearly. When previewing, you can still adjust font sizes, line spacing or the size and position of objects to get a better balanced page – all the normal menu commands are available and toolbars can be opened as needed.

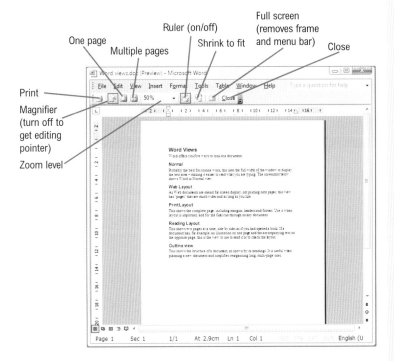

Full screen
(removes frame
Ruler (on/off)   and menu bar)
One page   Shrink to fit   Close
    Multiple pages

Print

Magnifier
(turn off to
get editing
pointer)

Zoom level

Timesaver tip

If you have an odd few lines on the last page, click Shrink to fit. This tries to fit the document onto one less page.

Getting Help

The simplest way to get Help is to ask for it. Type your question and Word will search through its Help system and offer you any topics that seem to be relevant.

If you have set up the Help options in Vista to use the online Help, then the search will include the system at Microsoft as well as the information stored in your own hard disk.

1 Type a question or one or more keywords in the Type a question for help box at the top right of the window.

2 The Search Results Task pane will open, and after a moment up to 30 matching topics will be listed.

If you are using the online Help, each topic will have two entries. The blue headings link to articles at Office Online; the grey ones take you to the Table of Contents (see page 74) at the relevant point.

If you are not using the online Help, the entries will all be in blue, and each links to an article in the Help system.

(see page 74)

Important

You don't actually need to type a properly worded question – simply giving one or more key words will do the job. 'custom bullets' will produce the same results as 'How do I customise bullets in a list?'

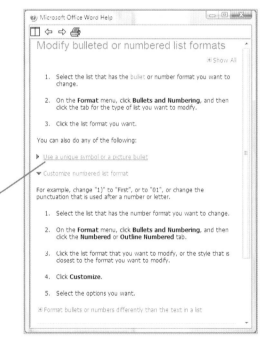

Getting Help (cont.)

3 Click a blue link to reach the Help page.

4 Headings with a blue arrowhead beside them are sets of instructions. Click on the heading to display the instructions.

Important

You can search for help online, offline or search for other things. Specify the type of search by picking an option from the drop-down list at the bottom of the Search Results pane.

Finding Help through the Contents

1. Open the Help menu and select Microsoft Office Word Help.

2. The Word Help task pane will open. In the top section, click the Table of Contents link.

If you are not sure which words to use to search for specific help, or if you want to browse to see what is available, have a look in the Table of Contents. Pick a heading (with a ✏ icon) and open that to see the page titles. Some sections have subsections, making it a two or three-stage process to get to page titles.

Some Help pages have a set of headings which you can open up to get detailed instructions on how to perform specific tasks.

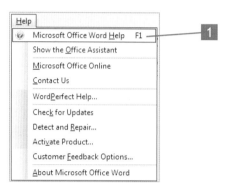

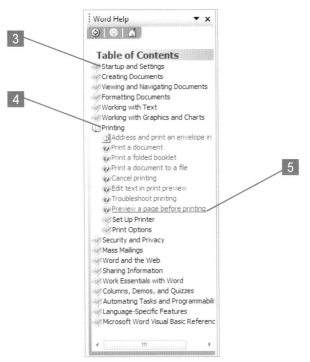

3　Click on a 🔖 to open up a section.

4　Click 📖 to close a section if it is not wanted.

5　Click on a heading with a a 📄 to display a Help page.

Did you know?

If you want a friendlier 'front-end' to the Help system – perhaps for the grandchildren if they use your PC – you can turn on the Office Assistant. This is an animated cartoon character which 'listens' to your questions and offers its answers. In practice it is exactly the same as using the Type a question box. To activate it, open the Help menu and select Show Office Assistant.

Managing your files

4

Introduction

To be able to use your computer efficiently, you must know how to manage your files – how to find, copy, move, rename and delete them – and how to organise the folders on your disks. In Windows Vista, the program that is used for file management is Windows Explorer. In this chapter we will see how it can be used for file and folder management. We will also look at creating links between documents and applications, and at the Recycle Bin – a neat device which makes it much less likely that you will delete files by accident.

The hard disk is the main place for storing files, but it is not the only one. Files can also be written on floppy disks and CD-ROM disks, for backup storage, or to move from one PC to another. We will be looking at these external storage media towards the end of the chapter.

What you'll do

Understand files and folders

Browse for files

Explore Windows Explorer

Customise the layout

View files

Customise the headings

Navigate with folders

Create a folder

Move folders

Set the folder type

Set Folder Options

Set search options

Use tags

Group files

Sort files

Filter files

Select files

Move and copy files

Rename files

Delete files

Use the Recycle Bin

Delete folders

Find files

Write to a CD

Understanding
files and folders

The hard disks supplied on modern PCs are typically 20 gigabytes or larger. 1 Gigabyte is 1 billion bytes and each byte can hold one character (or part of a number or of a graphic). That means that a typical hard disk can store nearly 4 billion words – enough for about 20,000 hefty novels! More to the point, if you were using it to store letters and reports, it could hold many, many thousands of them. Even if you are storing big audio or video files you are still going to get hundreds of them on the disk. It must be organised if you are ever to find your files.

Folders

Folders provide this organisation. They are containers in which related files can be placed to keep them together, and away from other files. A folder can also contain sub-folders – which can themselves by subdivided. You can think of the first level of folders as being sets of filing cabinets; those at the second level are drawers within the cabinets, and the next level are equivalent to divisions within the drawers. (And these could have subdividers too – there is no limit to this.)

You can just store all your files in My Documents, but it will get terribly crowded! It is a good idea to have a separate folder for each type of file, or each area of work, subdividing as necessary, so that no folder holds more than a few dozen files.

Paths

The structure of folders is often referred to as the tree. It starts at the root, which is the drive letter – C: for your main hard disk – and branches off from there.

A folder's position in the tree is described by its path. For most operations, you can identify a folder by clicking on it in a screen display, but now and then you will have to type its path. This should start at the drive letter and the root, and include every folder along the branch, with a backslash (\) between the names.

For example:
    C:\DTP
    C:\WordProcessing\Letters2007

When you want to know a path, look it up in the Explorer display and trace the branches down from the root.

Filenames

A filename has two parts – the name and an extension.

The name can be as long as you like, and include almost any characters – including spaces. But don't let this freedom go to your head. The longer the name, the greater the opportunity for typing errors. The most important thing to remember when naming a file is that the name must mean something to you, so that you can find it easily next time you want to use it.

The extension can be from 0 to 3 characters, and is separated from the rest of the name by a dot. It is used to identify the nature of the file. Windows uses the extensions COM, EXE, SYS, INI, DLL to identify special files of its own – handle these with care!

Most applications also use their own special extensions. Word-processor files are often marked with DOC; spreadsheet files are usually XLS; database files typically have DB extensions.

If you are saving a file in a word processor, spreadsheet or other application, and are asked for a filename, you normally only have to give the first part. The application will take care of the extension. If you do need to give an extension, make it meaningful. BAK is a good extension for backup files; TXT for text files.

When an application asks you for a filename – and the file is in the *current* folder – type in the name and extension only. If the file is in *another* folder, type in the path, a backslash separator and then the filename.

For example:

```
MYFILE.DOC
C:\WORPROC\REPORTS\MAY25.TXT
A:\MYFILE.BAK
```

Important

If there are several users, they will each have their own 'My Documents' folder set up by Windows Vista – any new folders should be created within this.

This is my Pictures folder. Most of my pictures are stored in the three folders: *basic*, *France* and *Vista*, but you will see a few unfiled images too.

Browsing for files

Don't worry too much about remembering paths. When you want to access a file in an application, you will usually be taken to an Open dialogue box in which you can select the drive, folder and file from a graphical display. Those that do not open this dialogue box directly will have a [Browse...] button to open it.

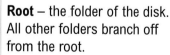

Important

In some older applications 'folders' are called 'directories'.

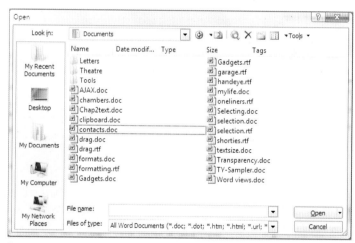

Browsing dialogue boxes from two applications.

Jargon buster

Root – the folder of the disk. All other folders branch off from the root.
Parent – a folder that contains another.
Child – a sub-folder of a Parent.
Branch – the structure of sub-folders that opens off from a folder.

Unlike every other Windows application, Windows Explorer (or Explorer for short) does not have its name in the title bar, and it is rarely started by name. The title bar displays the path to the folder that is open in Explorer, and the normal way of starting it is to open a folder.

The Explorer display can be varied in several ways. Some elements can be turned on or off, and some change in response to the material that is currently displayed. These four are always present:

- The Current Folder box shows you where you are now.
- The Search box can be used to hunt for a file (see page 106).
- The Toolbar buttons vary according to the type of folder or file that is selected at the time.
- The Contents pane usually shows the contents of the current folder. For Computer it shows the disks and other storage on the PC.

These are optional, though the first two are normally present:

- The Navigation pane has two parts: Favourite Links lets you open your most-used folders with one click; Folders shows the structure of folders (see page 87).
- The Details pane tells you the size, date and other details about the selected file or folder.
- The Preview pane shows a small version of an image or the first page of other documents, if a preview is available.
- The Search pane opens up when you run an advanced search (see page 107).
- The Menu bar gives another way to reach the commands and options.

If it has been turned on, the Status bar lies at the bottom of the window and shows the number of objects in the folder or the size of a selected file.

Exploring Windows Explorer

To start Explorer

Click .

Click Computer in the links on the right-hand side. This will run Explorer and open the Computer folder, which holds all the disk drives on your system.

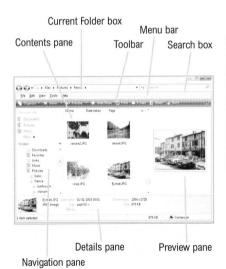

Current Folder box
Menu bar
Contents pane   Toolbar   Search box

Details pane   Preview pane
Navigation pane

Customising the layout

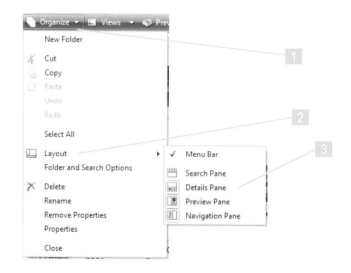

To turn the optional panes and Menu bar on or off:

1. Click on the Organise button.

2. Point to Layout.

3. Click on an element to toggle its display.

   If you turn on the Preview pane in Computer, there will be nothing to see. Let's find something else.

4. Click Documents in the Favourite Links list. Check that the Preview pane is present – it may not be, as Explorer opens each folder with the same display as was used previously. Turn it on if necessary.

5. Select a file and see if it has a preview.

6. The preview will be scaled to fit the Preview pane. If you want to change the size of the pane, drag on the divider.

Explorer can display files and folders in four views – List, Details, Tiles and Icons, and the icons can be anything from Small to Extra Large. The display is controlled through the Views button.

The Icons view shows a thumbnail of each file, if it can, and otherwise an icon to identify its type. It works best with images, but documents with previews can also be thumbnailed. The icons and thumbnails can be as large as you need to be able to identify files.

The List view is similar to Small Icons view, but packs more files into the same screen space.

Details gives a column display of properties under the headings Name, Type, Size, Tags, Date modified and others (these vary – see page 86). Every file has properties. Some of these are set by the system, e.g. its type and size; others can be changed by you, such as its name and where it is stored. Some properties are common to all types of files, but some types have additional properties.

Tiles displays a medium icon for each file, plus its name and other essential details.

Viewing files

To change the view

1. Click the Views button to cycle between the main types.

   or

2. Click the arrow beside the Views button to see the options.

3. Click on a name to select a view.

   or

4. Drag the slider to adjust the size – you can stop part-way between two set views to get an intermediate size.

4

Viewing files
(cont.)

Common file icons

 Bitmap image

 Web page

 Text

 Word document

 Excel workbook

 Open Type font

 System file – handle with care!

 Movie file

Zip compressed file

Tile view

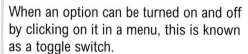

Did you know?

When an option can be turned on and off by clicking on it in a menu, this is known as a toggle switch.

For your information

Image icons are normally replaced by thumbnails of the image.

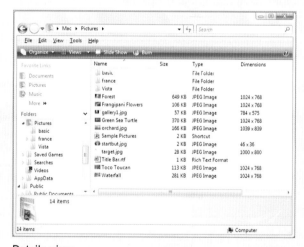

Details view

List view

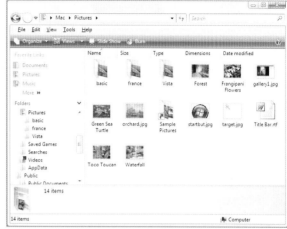

Medium icons view

Timesaver tip

If you turn on the Menu bar, you will have some additional layout and view options.

Customising the headings

You can choose which properties to include in the headings. This determines the properties that are displayed in Details view, but also affects the way that you can sort and group files in any view – see page 83.

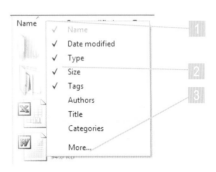

To customise the headings

1 Right-click anywhere along the headings. The menu lists the more important properties.

2 Click on a property name to toggle the tick on or off.

3 If you can't see the property you want to include, click More…

4 At the Choose Details dialogue box, tick the details you want to include.

5 The order of the columns in the display matches the order in this list. Select a detail and use the Move Up and Move Down buttons to rearrange its order if required.

6 Click OK.

The Folders display gives you easier ways to switch between folders, and to move files between them. It shows the disk drives, folders and network connections in a branching structure.

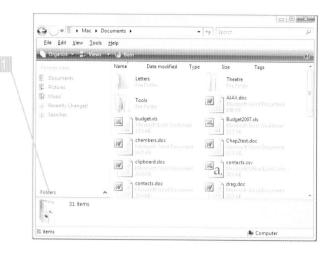

To use the Folders display

Click on the Folders bar, at the bottom of the Navigation pane, to open up the Folders display.

Click on any folder to select it. Its files and subfolders will be listed in the main pane.

A ▷ icon to the left of a folder name shows that the folder has subfolders. Click this to open up the branch.

The icon changes to ◢ . Click this to close the branch.

Creating a folder

Organised people set up their folders before they need them, so that they have places to store their letters – private and business, reports, memos, notes, and whatever, when they start to write them on their new system. They have a clear idea of the structure that they want, and create their folders at the right branches.

1 Select the folder that will be the parent of your new one, or the root if you want a new first-level folder.

2 Click the Organise button and select New Folder.

3 Replace 'New Folder' with a new name – any length, any characters, as with filenames.

Timesaver tip

If you want to change the name of a folder, right-click on it and select Rename, or use Rename this folder from the Common Tasks display.

Organised people may set up their folders before they create the documents that will go into them, but the rest of us set up our new folders when the old ones get so full that it is difficult to find things. Nor do we always create them in the most suitable place in the tree. Fortunately, Windows Vista caters for us too. Files can easily be moved from one folder to another, and folders can easily be moved to new places on the tree.

Here, Holiday photos is being moved from within Documents into Pictures, where it really belongs.

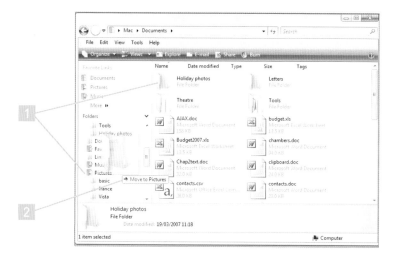

Moving folders

1 Arrange the display so that you can see the folder you want to move and the place it has to move to.

2 Drag the folder to its new position – the highlight will show you which one is currently selected.

See also

Moving and copying files, page 100.

Timesaver tip

Copying a folder – and all its files – to another disk can be a quick way to make a backup of a set of files.

Setting the folder type

Windows can be set to handle folders in slightly different ways if they hold pictures, sound or video files. This will affect the Tasks display – unless you have replaced these by Folders – and the default View setting.

1. In Computer, right-click on the folder.

2. Select Properties.

3. On the Customise tab pick a folder type to suit the contents.

Change the picture

4. If you want to change the image on the front of the folder, click Choose File… and browse for one.

Change the icon

5. If you want to change the icon used for the folder by Windows Explorer, click Change Icon…

6. Select the most suitable icon.

7. Click OK.

8. Back at the Properties dialogue box, click OK to save your settings.

These control the overall appearance of folders and the way that files are handled. The dialogue box has three tabs.

On the General tab there are three options:

▦ Select Show previews and filters to get the best out of Vista, or Use Windows classic folders for a simpler display.
▦ You can open each folder in a new window or in the same one.
▦ You can select items with a single or double-click.

The View panel controls the display of files. There are two main options here. The first is whether to show 'hidden' files. These are mainly found in the Windows and Windows/System folders. They are ones that you do not usually need to see and which are safer out of the way.

▦ Application extensions – files with .DLL extensions. They are used by applications and must not be deleted.
▦ System files – marked by .SYS after the name. These are essential to Windows' internal workings.
▦ Drivers – with .VXD or .DRV extensions. These make printers, screens and other hardware work properly.

The second key choice is whether you want to set different display styles for different folders – turn on Remember each folder's view settings if you do. If you have a mixture of styles already and want all folders to look the same, you can use the buttons to make them all look like the current folder or reset them all to their default settings.

The Search tab controls how Vista searches for files.

4

Setting Folder Options (cont.)

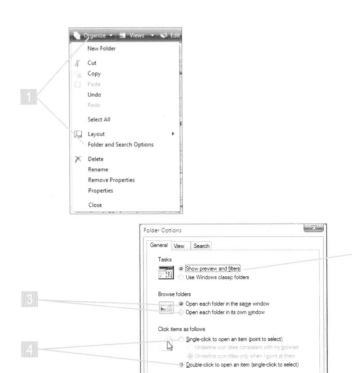

1. Click on the Organise button and select Folder and Search Options.

2. On the General panel select whether to Show previews and filters or Use Windows classic folders.

3. Set the Browse Folders option – the same or a new window?

4. Set the Click option.

5. Go to the View panel.

6. Click the checkbox to turn options on or off.

7. Click [Apply] to test the effect.

8. Click [OK].

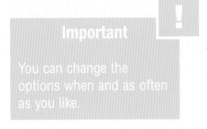

Important

You can change the options when and as often as you like.

If you want the same folder display throughout, click a button to use the current or the default settings

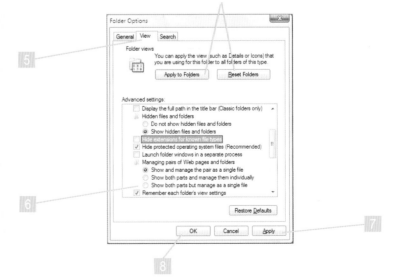

On the Search tab you can specify what, how and when to search. Vista creates indexes for your documents, based on the author, tags, and other properties. The default search routine looks through these indexes, and through the names of non-indexed files (mainly those of application and system programs).

Setting Search options

To set the options

1. In What to search, you can extend a search so that it also looks through the text of documents – very thorough, but rather slow, or restrict it to filenames – faster but you have to know some or all of the name.

2. In How to search, the key option is probably Find partial matches. If this is on, the search can find files based on a few letters of a name or tag – but note that this may find lots of irrelevant files that match those few letters.

3. In When searching non-indexed locations, you would not normally want to search the system folders, but if you have stored documents in compressed folders to save space, you may well want to search them.

Using tags

Tags are a type of property that can be used to sort, filter and group files in Explorer displays. They are handy for classifying digital photos, but they can help in any situation where a file can fit into several categories.

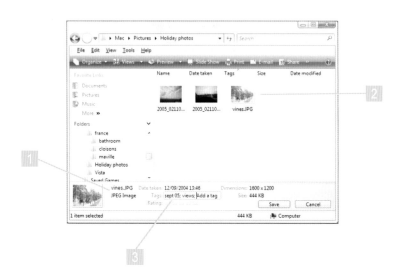

To add tags

1. Make sure that the Details pane is present in Explorer.

2. Select the file.

3. In the Details pane, click where it says Tags: Add a tag.

4. If this is the first time you have used the tag, type it in.

5. To add another tag, type a semicolon (;). Add a tag will reappear, and you can type in more.

6. Tags are stored by the system. If you want to add a tag that you have already used for other files, type the first letter or two. Any that contain the same letters will be listed below the Tags box – click one to select. It will be written in for you and 'Add a tag' will appear at the end again.

7. Press [Enter] or click Save to end.

8. If you want to remove a tag, select the file and click into the Tags box in the Details pane.

9. You cannot edit tags. If you decide one is not right, you must delete it and type a new one.

Important

Not all types of files can take tags. For example, you can add them to Word documents, other Microsoft Office files and JPGs (the standard digital photo format) but not to text files, BMP images or Web pages. If it doesn't say Tags in the Details pane, the file can't take them.

Explorer allows you to display files in groups. The groups can be based on any property shown in the headings, so you can group by type, or date, or tags. Tags have a unique effect on groups – if a file has more that one tag, it will be included in every matching group. This increases the number of items on display, but the grouping makes it simpler to find the ones you want.

Grouping files

To group files

Click the down arrow on the property you want to use.

Click the Group button at the top of the drop-down menu.

Scroll through, checking the name on the dividing lines.

Sorting files

Unless you specify otherwise, folders and files are listed in alphabetical order. Most of the time this works fine, but when you are moving or copying files, or hunting for them, other arrangements can be more convenient. You can sort them into order of name, type, size or the Date that they were last used.

To sort files

1. Open the View menu and point to Sort By.

2. Select Name, Size, Type, or Date modified.

   or

3. To sort by Name, Size, Type or Date, click on the column header.

4. Click on the header again to sort into reverse order.

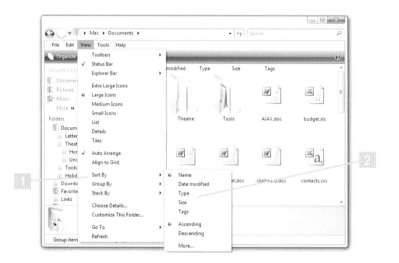

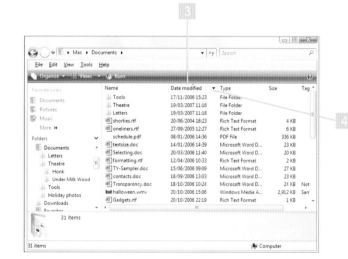

Timesaver tip

If the Menu bar is not displayed, right-click in the Content pane and select Sort By from the pop-up menu.

When you drop down the menu from a property heading, you will see the way files can be grouped – a list of tags or file types, alphabetical or size ranges, or whatever is appropriate to the property. You can use these same criteria to filter the display, so that only those files from selected groups are shown.

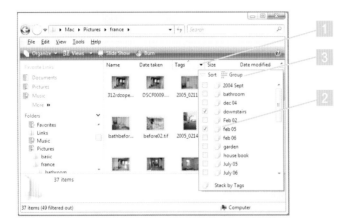

To filter files

1. Click the down arrow on the property you want to use.

2. Tick those groups that you want to include – the display will change to show the selected ones and hide the rest.

3. Click the Group button if you want to display the group headers.

4. Click anywhere off the menu to close it.

5. To restore the display so that all the files are included, you can either tick every box in the list or clear the ticks from them all – do which ever takes the fewest clicks!

Did you know?

Obviously names are unique, so you can't use them for grouping – instead files are grouped by alphabetical ranges. In the same way, size ranges can be used for grouping.

Selecting files

You can easily select one file by clicking on it, but you can also select sets of files. This is useful when you want to back up a day's work, by copying the new files to a disk, or move a set from one folder to another or delete a load of unwanted files.

You can select:

- a block of adjacent files
- a scattered set
- the whole folder-full.

The same techniques work with all display styles.

To select a block using the mouse

1. Point to one corner of the block and click.
2. Drag an outline over the ones you want.

To [Shift] select

3. Click on the file at one end of the block.
4. If necessary, scroll the window to bring the other end into view.
5. Hold [Shift].
6. Click on the far end file.

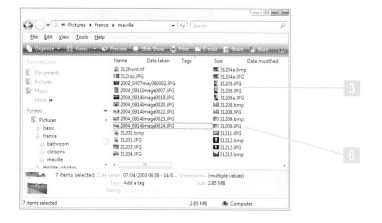

Timesaver tip

It may be easier to arrange icons by Name, Date or Type, before you start to select.

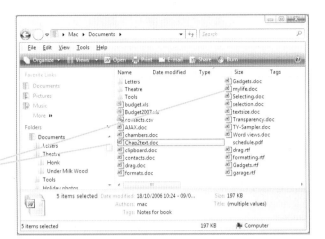

Selecting files (cont.)

To select scattered files

7 Click on any one of the files you want.

8 Hold [Control] and click on each of the other files.

9 You can deselect any file by clicking on it a second time.

To select all the files

10 Click on the Organise button.

11 Choose Select All.

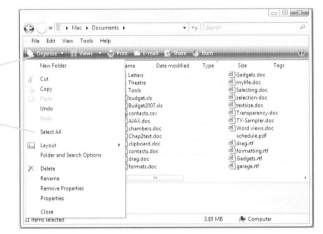

Timesaver tip

If you have the Menu bar displayed and you want all the files except for a scattered few, select those few, then use Edit, Invert Selection to deselect them and select the others.

4

Moving and copying files

When you drag a file from one place to another, the file will either move or be copied. In general:

- It moves if you drag it to somewhere on the same disk.
- It is copied if you drag the file to a different disk.

When you are dragging files within a disk, you are usually moving to reorganise your storage; and copying is most commonly used to create a safe backup on a separate disk.

If you want to move a file from one disk to another, or copy within a disk, hold down the right mouse button while you drag. A menu will appear when you reach the target folder. You can select Move or Copy from there.

1. Select the file(s).

2. Scroll the Folders list so that you can see the target folder – don't click on it!

3. Point to any one of the selected files and drag to the target.

   or

4. Hold down the right mouse button while you drag then select Move or Copy.

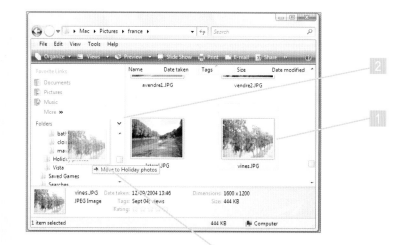

Timesaver tip

The easiest way to copy a file to a disk is to right-click on it to open its Context menu, then point to Send To and select the disk drive.

100

If you are having difficulty arranging the Explorer display so that you can see the source files and the target folder, the simplest approach is to use the Move To Folder or Copy To Folder commands. These let you pick the target folder through a dialogue box.

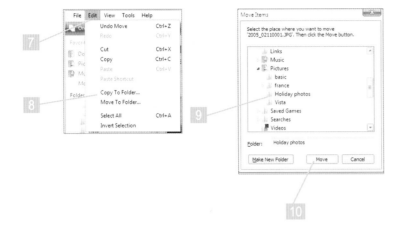

Moving and copying files (cont.)

Move To Folder/Copy To Folder

5 If the Menu bar is not displayed, open it now.

6 Select the file(s).

7 Open the Edit menu.

8 Select Copy To or Move To Folder.

9 Select the target drive or folder.

10 Click Move or Copy.

Timesaver tip

You can use the Cut, Copy and Paste commands to move and copy files and folders. Find them on the Edit menu, or on the Context menu when you right-click on a file or in a folder.

Copy stores a copy of the file or folder in the Clipboard.

Cut removes the original file, storing a copy in the Clipboard.

Paste puts a copy of the stored file into the current folder.

Renaming files

You can rename a file if necessary – and it may well be necessary if the original name was created automatically by a program, as happens when you import images from a digital camera into the PC.

1. Select the file you want to rename.

2. Press [F2] on your keyboard.

   or

3. Click on the Organise button or open the right-click menu and select Rename.

4. Edit the name as required and press [Enter] to fix the new name.

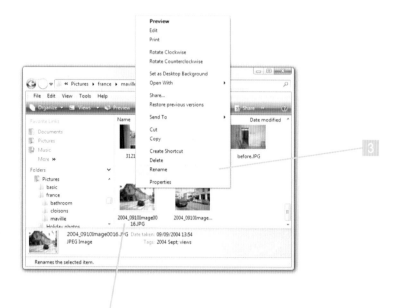

In the earlier days of computing, it was all too easy to delete a file by mistake, wiping out hours or days – or even weeks – of work. Windows protects you from yourself! When you delete a file, it is not immediately erased from the hard disk. Instead it is taken from its folder and placed in the Recycle Bin, from which it can easily be recovered.

Select the file, or group of files.

Right-click and select Delete.

or

Press [Delete].

At the Confirm prompt, click Yes or No to confirm or stop the deletion. With single deletions, the filename is displayed; with multiple deletions you just get the number of selected files.

Important

Floppy disks are different from hard disks. If you delete a file from a floppy it really does get wiped out!

Using the Recycle Bin

This is a wonderful feature, especially for those of us given to making instant decisions that we later regret. Until you empty the Bin, any 'deleted' files and folders can be instantly restored – and if the folder that they were stored in has also been deleted, that is re-created first, so things go back into their proper place.

Files sent to the Recycle Bin stay there until you empty it. You should do this regularly, to free up disk space.

To restore files

1. Open the Recycle Bin from the icon on the desktop or from Windows Explorer.

2. Select the files that were deleted by mistake – the Original Location field shows you where they were.

3. Right-click for the Context menu and select Restore or click Restore the items in the toolbar.

To empty the bin

4. Check that there is nothing that you want, and restore any files if necessary.

5. Select Empty Recycle Bin from the toolbar.

Timesaver tip

You can delete folders or files by dragging them directly to the Recycle Bin.

This is not something you will do every day, for deleting a folder also deletes its files, and files are usually precious things. But we all acquire programs we don't need, keep files long past their use-by dates, and sometimes create unnecessary folders.

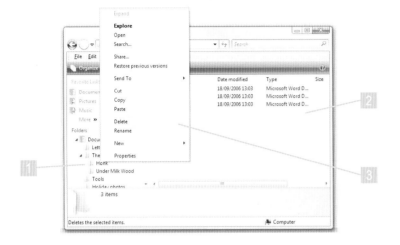

1. Select the folder.

2. Check the files list. Are there any there? Do you want any of them? No, then carry on.

3. Right-click on the folder to open the Context menu or click the Organise button and select Delete.

4. If necessary, you can stop the process by clicking No when you are asked to confirm that the folder is to be thrown in the Bin.

Important

If you delete a folder by mistake it can be restored from the Recycle Bin.

Finding files

Windows Explorer has a neat Search utility, which can track down lost files for you, hunting for them by name, location, tags, contents, date, type and/or size.

A simple search can use all or part of the filename, or the content of text files (in indexed folders). Here's how to find a file if you can remember what it was called, or a keyword in it, but not where you stored it.

To find files

1. In the Folders or Favourites list, select the highest level folder that you think it could be in. The search routine will go through all the subfolders.

2. Click into the Search box and type all or part of the name or of a significant word. Almost as soon you start to type, the search results will be displayed in the Contents pane. Type more of the filename, and the results will be filtered further, reducing the number of matching files.

3. Double-click on the file to open it, or make a note of its folder so that you can find it easily again later.

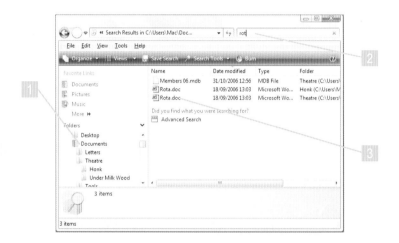

If the simple search doesn't find the file you can use Advanced Search.

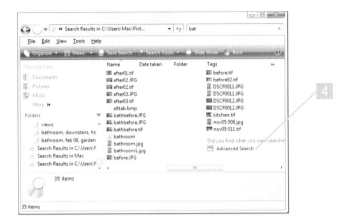

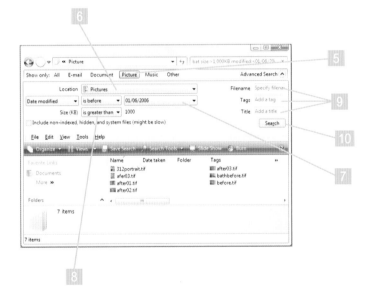

To use the Advanced Search

4 Click the Advanced Search link at the bottom of the results.

5 In the Show only bar at the top, select the type of file you are looking for.

6 In the Location options, select the highest-level folder, or the disk drive, or Everywhere if you haven't a clue where it might be.

7 To filter by Date, select Date modified, Date created or Date accessed, then select Is and set the range, or Is before/after and set the date.

8 To filter by Size, select equals, Is less than or Is greater than and set the limit.

9 Type part or all of the filename, tags or title.

10 Click Search.

Writing to a CD

CDs come in three varieties:

A CD-ROM is read-only memory. You can read data from this kind of CD, but you cannot write it onto it. Applications software is normally supplied on CD-ROM nowadays.

A CD-W disk is writeable – you can store data on it. But this is a one-off thing. Once you have written data onto it, you cannot change what is stored there, or add more data.

A CD-R disk is rewriteable – you can store data on it, but you can add more data later, or update the files stored there. The only limitation is this: writing really is a once-only process – it changes the surface of the disk irredeemably. When you erase something from the disk, or replace a file with a newer copy, you cannot reuse the space which had been occupied by the old file. With reuse, CD-R gradually fills up.

1 In Windows Explorer, locate the files you want to write to the CD.

2 Place a blank or part-used CD in the drive. Wait for Windows to read the disk. You may be asked what you want Windows to do. The answer is to burn files to disk.

Writing to a CD (cont.)

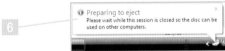

Enter a title for the disk, to identify it, and click Next.

You may be asked to confirm that you want to format the disk – you do. It will take a few moments.

A second Explorer window will open, showing the CD drive. Drag files from the first Explorer window and drop them in here. You can move them one at a time, or in groups – whichever is easiest.

Press the button to eject the CD from the drive. A message will appear telling you that Windows is preparing to eject. Wait while the files are written to the CD. This is slower than writing to a hard drive, so be patient. When the files are written, the drive will open and the CD can be removed.

Did you know?

Most new PCs can also write to DVDs in exactly the same way as they can to CDs. Since they can store far more – 6 or 7 Gigabytes, rather than 700 Megabytes – you would normally only use them for backing up the whole system, or for storing video files.

Further word processing

Introduction

You can do so much more with Word than simply type and edit text. Word has full page layout facilities – so much so that people sometimes use it to produce books. (Though in truth, it's not the software that most typesetters use if they have any choice!) But it is regularly used to produce newsletters, brochures, greetings cards, menus, advertisements and all manner of documents where appearance and style matter.

In this chapter we will explore some of Word's more advanced formatting and layout facilities. Try them out. Some you will never use again, but some you will find very handy.

And do check out the mail merge. You can save yourself a lot of time and effort next Christmas if you use mail merge to produce the labels for the cards' envelopes – or even, dare I suggest it, to personalise that 'roundup of the year' that you send out with the cards.

Formatting with the Font dialogue box

If you want to set several font options at the same time – perhaps to make a heading larger, bold and in a different font – or you want to set one of the less-used options, you can use the Font dialogue box. Here's how.

1. Select the text to be formatted.

2. Open the Format menu and select Font…

3. At the Font dialogue box, make sure that you are on the Font tab.

4. Set the font, style, size and/or other options as required.

5. Check the Preview and adjust the settings if necessary.

6. Click OK.

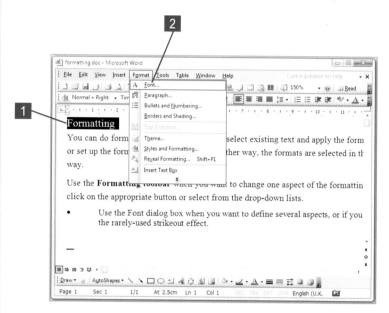

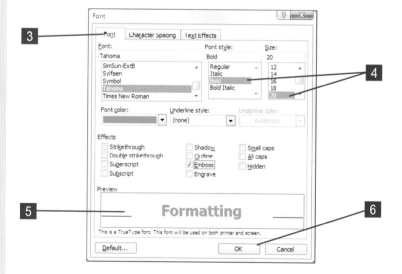

Line spacing refers to the amount of vertical space between lines of text. The default is for single spacing, which is fine for most purposes. If you need more space, either to create a particular visual effect or to leave room for people to add notes on the printout, then it can be set to 1.5 lines, double spacing or other specific settings.

The spacing can only be set through the Paragraph dialogue box.

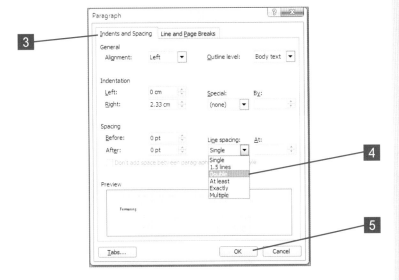

Setting the line spacing

1 Select the paragraph(s).

2 Open the Format menu and select Paragraph.

3 Bring the Indents and Spacing tab to the front.

4 Open the Line spacing list and select the level.

5 Click OK.

! Important

Line spacing can only be applied to whole paragraphs. Remember that a paragraph is selected if any part of it is selected or it contains the insertion point.

5

Indenting text

Indents set the distance from the edge of the page margins of your text. They can also be used to create a structure of headings and subheadings.

The left indent can be set with the toolbar buttons – each click pushes the text in (or out) 5mm. If you want to indent from the right, or set a different left indent on the first line, you need to use the Paragraph dialogue box.

1 Select the text.

2 Click 📑 to increase the indent.

or

3 Click 📑 to pull back out.

or

4 Open the Format menu and select Paragraph.

5 Go to the Indents and Spacing tab.

6 Type values, or use the scroll arrows to set the Left and/or Right indents.

7 To set a different indent for the first line, drop-down the Special list and select First Line or Hanging, then set the distance.

8 Click OK .

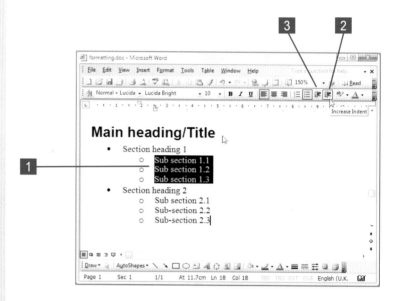

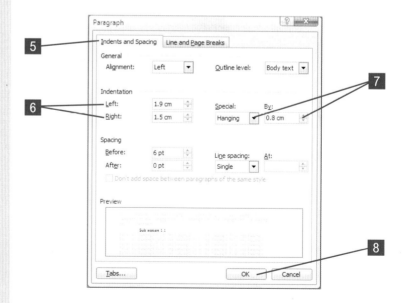

Though Indents can be set more accurately by typing values into the Indents and Spacing tab of the Paragraph dialogue box, it is quicker and simpler to use the indent markers on the ruler.

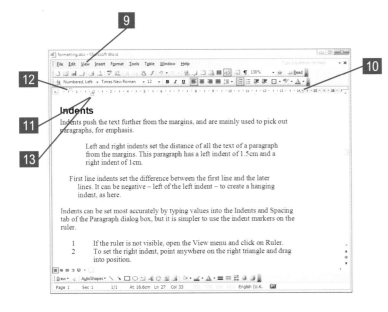

Setting indents with the ruler

9 If the ruler is not visible, open the View menu and click on Ruler.

10 To set the right indent, point anywhere on the right triangle and drag into position.

11 To set the left indent, drag on the lower left triangle.

12 To set the first line indent, drag on the upper left triangle.

13 To move the left and first line indents together, drag on the square beneath the left indent triangle.

5

Setting tabs

If you are writing a price list, CV or similar where text or figures need to be in accurate columns, you should use tabs.

By default, the tabs are at ½ inch (1.2 cm) intervals and left aligned. The position and the style of the tabs can be easily changed.

When you press [Tab], the insertion point moves to the next tab position, pushing any existing text across with it.

Tab styles

⌐ Left edge of the text aligns with the tab.

⊥ Text centres on the tab.

⌐ Right edge of the text aligns with the tab.

⊥ Decimal points align with the tab.

| Bar tab draws a vertical line at the tab point.

Setting tabs

1 If the ruler is not present, open the View menu and tick Ruler.

2 Select the text for which you want to set tabs.

3 The current tab style is shown at the left of the ruler. To change the style, keep clicking the icon until you see the style you want.

4 Click on the ruler to place the tab. The default ½ inch interval tabs to its left will be removed.

5 To move a tab, click on it and drag it into a new position.

6 Repeat steps 3 to 5 to set any other tabs for the selected block of text.

7 Click anywhere in the working area to deselect the text.

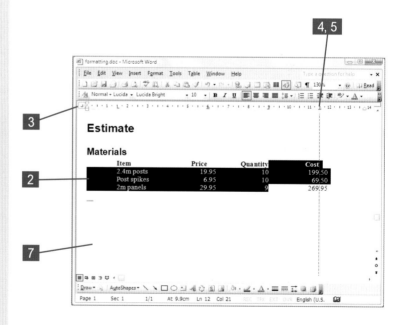

A style is a combination of font, size, alignment and indent options. Word has a range of pre-defined styles, and you can modify these or add your own. Applying a style is a matter of a couple of clicks; creating a new style is almost as simple.

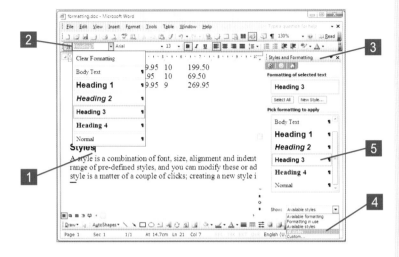

To apply a style

1 Select the text – normally one or more whole paragraphs.

2 Pick a style from the drop-down Styles list.

or

3 Open the Format menu and select Styles and Formatting... to open the styles list in the Task pane.

4 In the Show box, select All styles.

5 Pick from the long list.

! Important

Most styles are intended to be applied to whole paragraphs; others are 'character styles' which are designed for use with selected pieces of text.

5

Working with styles (cont.)

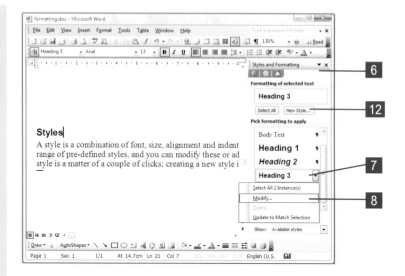

To modify a style

6 Open Styles and Formatting in the Task pane.

7 Pick a style.

8 Click its down arrow and select Modify.

9 Edit the main format settings if required.

10 For more extensive changes, click the Format button and select an aspect to open its dialogue box.

11 Click ⌑ OK ⌑.

To create a style

12 At the Style dialogue box, click ⌑ New Style... ⌑.

13 For the Style type, select Character if you want to use this on selected text within a paragraph, otherwise select Paragraph.

14 Type in a Name then follow steps 3 to 6.

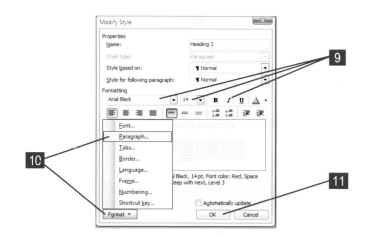

You can quickly add numbers or bullets to each item in a list by clicking 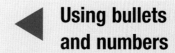 or ⟦≣⟧. This will set the default bullet or number style, but these defaults can easily be changed if you want to give your list a special look.

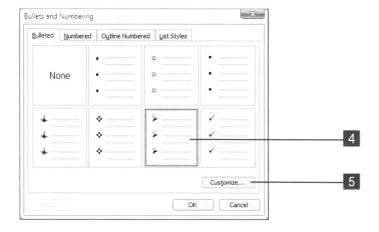

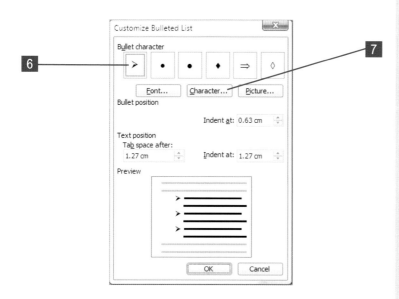

To add or remove bullets

1 Select the list and click ⟦≣⟧. If the list already has bullets, this will remove them.

To modify bullets

2 Reselect the list.

3 Open the Format menu or right-click to open the Context menu and select Bullets and Numbering.

4 Select a style.

5 Click ⟦Customize...⟧.

6 Pick a bullet style.

or

7 Click ⟦Character...⟧ to choose a different character.

5

Using bullets and numbers (cont.)

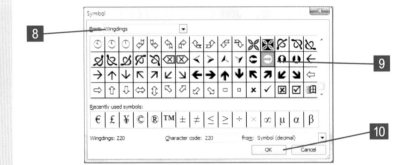

8 Select a font and subset (if required).

9 Select a character.

10 Click OK.

Important

Word may be set to produce numbered or bulleted lists automatically – these are AutoFormatting options. See page 124.

Headers and footers appear at the top and bottom of every page. They can display the page number, date and time, filename, author and similar file details, or any typed text.

The page number, date, and other details can be produced by field codes. These are replaced by the appropriate information when inserted into the pages, and are updated as necessary. For example, the Page # field code produces the correct page number on each page.

The header and footer have tabs in place so that items can go on the left, centre or right.

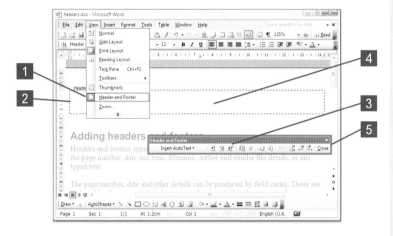

Header/footer tools

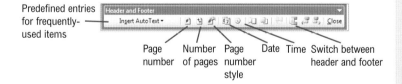

Predefined entries for frequently-used items

Page number · Number of pages · Page number style · Date · Time · Switch between header and footer

1 Open the View menu and select Header and Footer. The header always appears first. If you want to start in the footer, click 🗐 on the Header and Footer toolbar.

2 Type your text.

or

3 Select a field code from the Header and Footer toolbar.

4 Press [Tab] to move to the centre or right and repeat if required.

5 Click Close to go to the normal page view.

Timesaver tip

If you can't work out what the icons on the Header and Footer toolbar mean – and some are not very obvious – pause the mouse over the tool to see the tool tip.

5

Correcting errors automatically

Word likes to be helpful. You can get it to watch your typing and correct some common errors as they occur. For instance, I routinely type 'hte' when I mean 'the', but Word knows what I mean and it will replace my mistyped text with the correct word as soon as I have finished it. (Which means that I have to trick it if I actually want to write 'hte'.)

You can select which sorts of errors to correct, and add your own common typos to its list of corrections.

1 Open the Tools menu and select AutoCorrect Options.

2 On the AutoCorrect tab, tick those checkboxes where you want Word to make the correction.

3 If you turn on Replace as you type, you can add your own typos. Put the expected typo in the Replace field, and what you want to replace it with in the With field.

4 Click Replace.

5 Click OK.

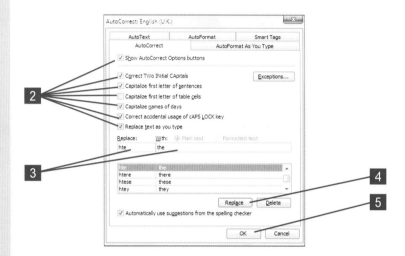

Timesaver tip

If there are any long names or phrases which you use regularly, e.g. the name of your football team, you could add them to your AutoCorrect list, using initials or shortforms in the Replace field. Then next time you are writing a letter to a chum complaining about their performance at the last match, you could just type WW each time instead of Wolverhampton Wanderers (or whatever).

Word can also reformat things properly as you type. For example, it can turn fractions typed like this 1/2 into special fraction characters like this ½. Or when you start to type a numbered list, it can take over the numbering for you after the first line. The options are on the AutoFormat As You Type tab of the AutoCorrect dialogue box.

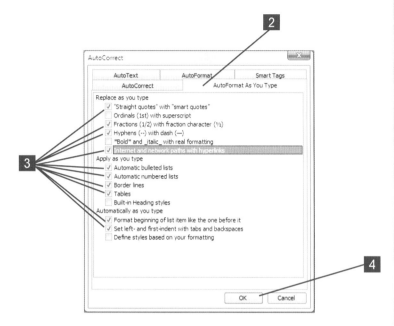

1 Open the Tools menu and select AutoCorrect Options.

2 Switch to the AutoFormat As You Type tab.

3 Tick those checkboxes where you want Word to apply formatting as you type, or to replace characters as they are typed.

4 Click OK.

5

Using AutoFormats

1. Open the Format menu and select AutoFormat.
2. Select AutoFormat and review.
3. Click OK.

When word processors added facilities for fancy fonts and layouts, productivity in many offices took a great leap backwards. Instead of simply typing and printing their documents, people spent time – often too much – prettying them up. Not enough people asked themselves if it was really worth the effort. The trouble is, if you want your documents to look 'professional', plain typing will no longer do. But don't worry, here's a great leap forward. Word can format your documents for you, giving a professional result, instantly.

Just to confuse you, Word calls this AutoFormatting, and it is not the same as the AutoFormatting that corrects and replaces as you type!

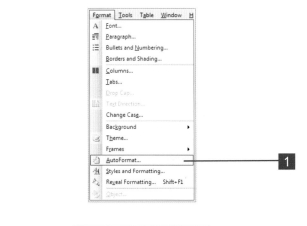

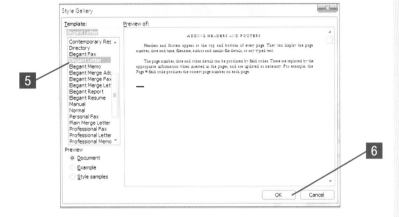

4 When you get the Formatting completed message, click Style Gallery.

5 At the Style Gallery, select a style, checking it in the preview screen.

6 Click OK when you find one you like.

7 Click Review changes.

8 Use the Find buttons to work through the changes and Reject any you don't like.

9 Click Cancel to end the review.

10 Click Accept All.

5

Checking your spelling

Word, like all modern applications that handle text, has a spell checker that compares your words with those in its dictionary. Word comes supplied with a good dictionary, but it does not cover everything. Proper names, technical and esoteric words may not be recognised and so will be classed as 'errors'. These can be added to your own custom dictionary, so that they are not seen as errors in future.

Word has a Check spelling as you type option. You may prefer to just run a spell check after you have finished – especially if you have a lot to do and need to watch the keyboard rather than the screen!

1 If you want to check part of a document, select it before starting the spell check.

2 Open the Tools menu and select Spelling and Grammar or click [✓].

When a word is not in the dictionary you can

3 Select a suggestion from the list and click [Change].

or

4 If it is a valid word click [Ignore Once] or [Ignore All].

or

5 Click [Add to Dictionary] to put it in a custom dictionary.

or

6 Click in the Not in Dictionary slot, and edit the word then click on [Change].

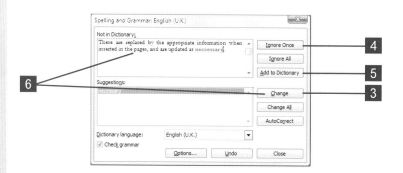

Timesaver tip

If you haven't already set up a dictionary for your own special words, click the Options button to open the Spelling options panel and use the Custom Dictionaries button.

Word can check the grammar of a document as well as its spelling, and for both spelling and grammar there are a number of options that you can set to adjust the way they work. Probably the key option is whether or not to check as you type – some people will find that it interrupts their flow.

To set Spelling options

1 On the Spelling dialogue box, click Options.

2 Turn the settings on or off as desired.

To set Grammar options

3 Click [Settings...].

4 In Writing style, select Grammar Only or Grammar and Style.

5 Turn other checks on or off as desired.

6 Click [OK].

Did you know?

Word can tell you the 'readability' level of a document. A readability of Grade 7 (a reading age of 12) is a good level for an adult audience – any lower is patronising, but higher is hard work for most people. The *Daily Mail* newspaper has a reading age of 12; the *Sun's* reading age is around 8.

5

Applying borders and shading

Borders and shading can be very good ways to emphasise items in a document. They are normally applied to whole paragraphs, though there is nothing to stop you adding a border or a background shade – or both – to a word or phrase within a paragraph.

Borders can be applied and formatted using the Tables and Borders toolbar – but note that you must set the formats first. You can change the formatting after the border is in place using the Borders and Shading dialogue box. This has some additional formatting options.

To add a border

1. Select the text or paragraph(s).

2. Click the Tables and Borders tool on the Standard toolbar to display the Tables and Borders toolbar.

3. The Draw Table tool will be selected – click on it to switch it off.

4. Choose the Line Style, Weight and Colour required.

5. Click the arrow beside the Borders tool to display the bordering options.

6. Click an icon to select which sides the border is to be applied to. Note that the inside options only apply to tables.

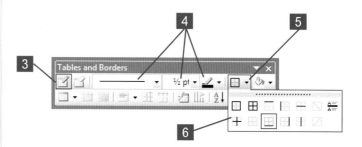

To format an existing border

7. Select the bordered text.

8. Open the Format menu and select Borders and Shading…

9. Bring the Borders tab to the front.

10. Choose a Setting – Box, Shadow or 3-D.

11. Set the line Style, Colour and Width.

12. Click OK.

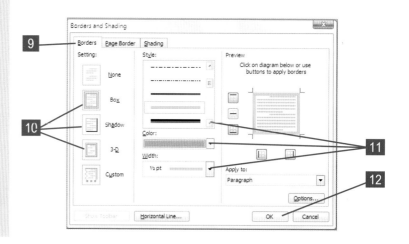

You can apply Shading to selected text or whole paragraphs, using the tool on the Tables and Borders toolbar and the tab in the Borders and Shading dialogue box.

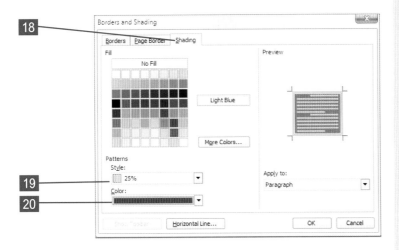

To remove a border

13 Select the text or paragraph(s).

14 Display the Borders toolbar.

15 Open the border options palette and click No Border to remove the existing borders.

To add shading

16 Select the text or paragraph(s) you wish to add shading to.

17 To set a simple colour, click the down arrow beside the Shading tool and pick one from the palette.

or

18 If you want a patterned shade, open the Format menu, select Borders and Shading… and switch to the Shading tab.

19 Set the pattern style, e.g. Lt Dwn (Light Down) Diagonal.

20 Pick the colour.

5

Did you know?

If you need a fancy line to mark off a section in a document, you will find a selection in the Horizontal Line options in the Borders and Shading dialogue box. Click the Horizontal Line… button and pick one to suit.

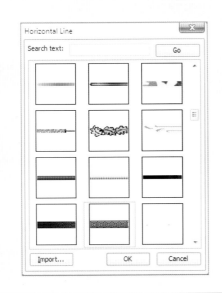

Applying a page border

If you are producing a poster, brochure, certificate or similar document, you might want to add a border around the whole page. This is easily done.

1 Open the Format menu, select Borders and Shading.

2 Switch to the Page Border tab.

3 Define the Style, Colour and Width of the line, as for other borders.

or

4 Select a decorative border from the Art drop down list.

5 If you do not want the border on certain sides, click on their icons in the Preview area.

6 Click OK.

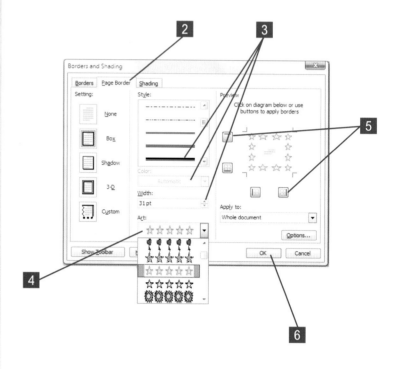

If you need to lay out data in neat columns and rows, the simplest way to do this is with a table.

If you want to create a simple regular table, use the 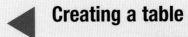 button on the Standard toolbar or the Table, Insert, Table command. Whatever size you set at the start is not fixed – rows and columns can be added or deleted later.

The AutoFit behaviour sets how the table fits around its contents and within the window.

- Fixed column width – the widths stay the same unless you change them.
- AutoFit to contents – the columns shrink or stretch so that they match the contents.
- AutoFit to window – the table adjusts to fit the width of the page or screen (useful if you are using Word to create a web page).

1. Place the cursor where the table is to go.
2. Click 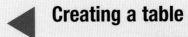 and drag the highlight across the grid to set the size, and go to step 8.

   or
3. Use the Table, Insert, Table... command.
4. At the Insert Table dialogue box set the number of rows and columns.
5. Choose an AutoFit behaviour.
6. Click AutoFormat.

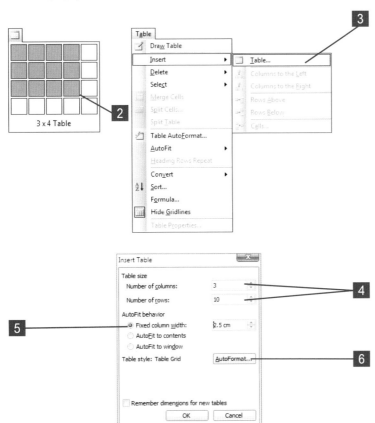

5

Creating a table (cont.)

7 Select a design from the dialogue box if you want to apply a ready-made format.

8 Enter the data into the cells, formatting the text if required.

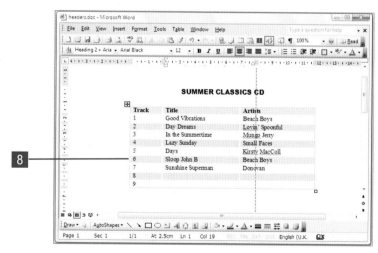

Timesaver tip

The AutoFormats cover all aspects of formatting, but you do not have to apply them all – turn off those aspects that you don't want.

Text in cells within tables can be formatted as normal. You can also:

- Set the vertical and horizontal alignment of cell contents.
- Format the borders and the lines within the table – this is slightly tricky.
- Change the background colour.

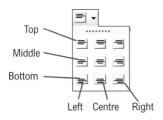

Top
Middle
Bottom

Left   Centre   Right

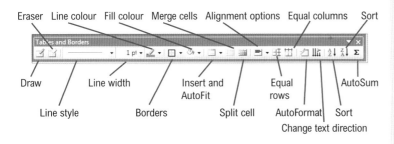

Eraser   Line colour   Fill colour   Merge cells   Alignment options   Equal columns   Sort

Draw   Line width   Insert and   Equal   AutoSum
                              AutoFit   rows

Line style   Borders   Split cell   AutoFormat   Sort

Change text direction

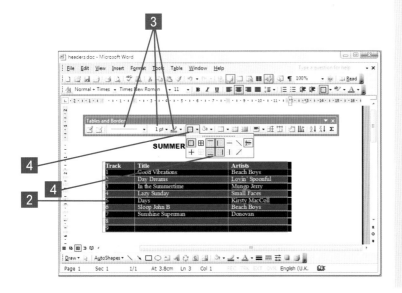

To set borders

1 Open the View menu, point to Toolbars and turn on the Tables and Borders toolbar.

2 Select the cells.

3 Set the line style, width and colour.

4 Click the Border tool and select the lines to be styled.

5

Further word processing 133

Modifying a table

A table's size, shape and layout can be changed at any time – even after data has been entered into it. You can:

- Insert or delete rows or columns.
- Change the width of columns.
- Change the overall size of the table.

To insert a row or column

1 Click into a cell in the row or column adjacent to where the new one will go.

2 Select an Insert option from the Table menu.

To delete rows or columns

3 Click into a cell in the row or column, or drag across (or down) the table to select two or more rows or columns.

4 Select a Delete option from the Table menu.

To change the column width

5 Point to the dividing line on the right of a column to get the double-headed arrow, then drag the line left or right to set the width.

or

6 Drag on the column marker on the ruler.

To change the table size

7 Point to a corner so the cursor becomes the resize arrow, then drag the table outline to the required size.

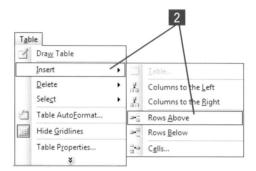

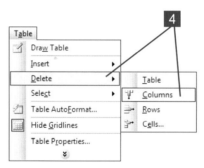

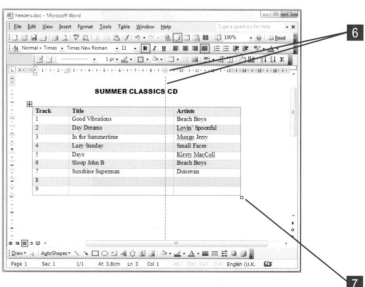

Some characters cannot be typed directly from the keyboard, but that doesn't mean that you cannot use them in your documents. You just have to get them from another source. The Insert Symbol routine lets you access the untypeable!

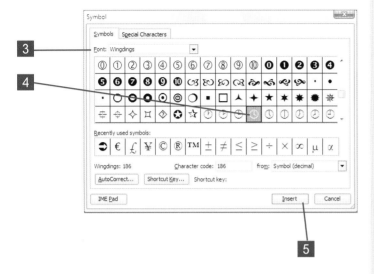

1 Place the insertion point where you want the character to go.

2 Open the Insert menu and select Symbol.

3 Pick a font from the list – you will find the biggest choice of symbols and graphics in the Symbol, Wingding and Webding fonts.

4 Click on a character to see an enlargement.

5 Click Insert to insert the selected character into your text.

6 Click ✕ to close the Symbol dialogue box.

Did you know?

There is a collection of special characters on the other tab in the Symbol dialogue box. These are mainly used in professional typesetting.

5

Inserting pictures

Word can handle graphics files in many formats including BMP, JPG, GIF, Photo CD and possibly many more, depending upon which graphic converter routines have been installed. The pictures may have been captured by a scanner or digital camera, downloaded from the web, or drawn in a graphics program.

1 Open the Insert menu, point to Picture then select From File.

or

2 Click 🖾 on the Picture toolbar.

3 Switch to the picture's folder.

4 The folder should be in Thumbnails view. Preview gives a slightly better look at one file at a time. Switch to this if it will help.

5 Click on a picture.

6 Click Insert.

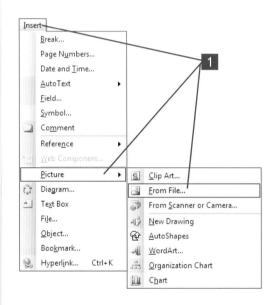

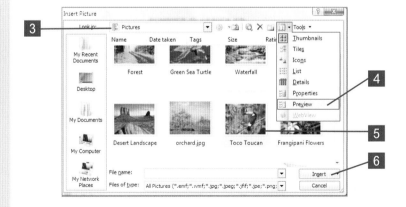

Clip art pictures can be inserted into any application – but don't overdo it. There's so much clip art around that you must use it selectively to have any impact.

Clip art is accessed through the Task pane.

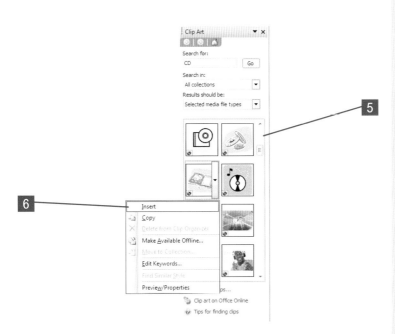

Inserting clip art

1 Use Insert, Picture, Clip Art… to open Clip Art in the Task pane.

2 Type the Search for word(s).

3 Drop down the Results should be menu. List and tick the types of media that you want.

4 Click Go.

5 Scroll through the results to find a picture.

6 To insert the image, double-click or click the arrow bar and select Insert.

7 Close the Task pane if no longer required.

Timesaver tip

You can preview sounds, video clips, animated GIFs and similar files in the ClipArt Task pane.

5

Formatting pictures

The final appearance of any picture – file or clip art – can be adjusted at any point. Use the mouse to change the size, shape or position, or use the Picture toolbar or the right-click menu to add a border or caption, to crop it, adjust the colours, or set how text wraps around it.

1 Select the picture.

2 Drag a handle to adjust the size.

3 Drag anywhere within the area to move the whole picture.

4 Use the Picture tools to adjust the settings.

5 Right-click for the Context menu and use its options to add a border or caption.

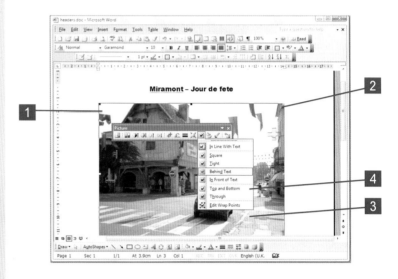

The Picture toolbar

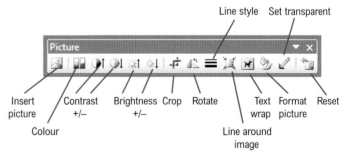

Line style Set transparent

Insert picture   Contrast +/−   Brightness +/−   Crop   Rotate   Text wrap   Format picture   Reset

Colour   Line around image

Image control options

Automatic – in its normal colours.

Grayscale – for output to black-only printers.

Black & White – for high-contrast printing, use with line-drawings or for special effects.

Watermark – ultra-pale, for use as backgrounds.

Cut
Copy
Paste
Edit Picture
Hide Picture Toolbar
Borders and Shading...
Caption...
Format Picture...
Hyperlink...

If you want to create new images, pick out points on imported pictures, or add arrows, blobs or blocks of background colour, there is a handy set of tools on the Drawing toolbar.

In a drawn picture, each item remains separate and can be moved, resized, recoloured or deleted at any later time. (Though items can be joined into Groups or placed inside picture frames, for convenient handling.) This is quite different from Paint and similar packages, where each addition becomes merged permanently into the whole picture.

Drawing pictures

1 Click [ ] to open the Drawing toolbar.

2 Select an object tool and point and drag to create the item.

3 Adjust the fill and line colour and style.

4 To adjust an item, use the Selector tool and click on it. It can then be moved, resized, deleted or recoloured.

5 Double-click on an element to open its Format dialogue box for fine-tuning its display.

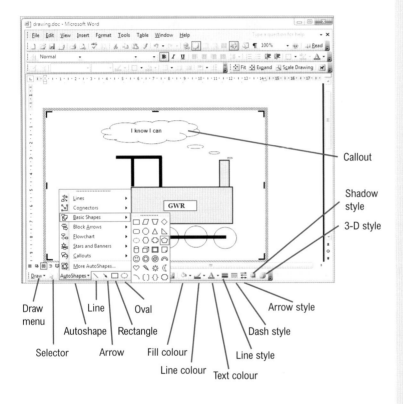

Callout

Shadow style

3-D style

Arrow style

Dash style

Draw menu

Line

Oval

Autoshape

Rectangle

Line style

Selector

Arrow

Fill colour

Line colour

Text colour

5

Drawing
pictures (cont.)

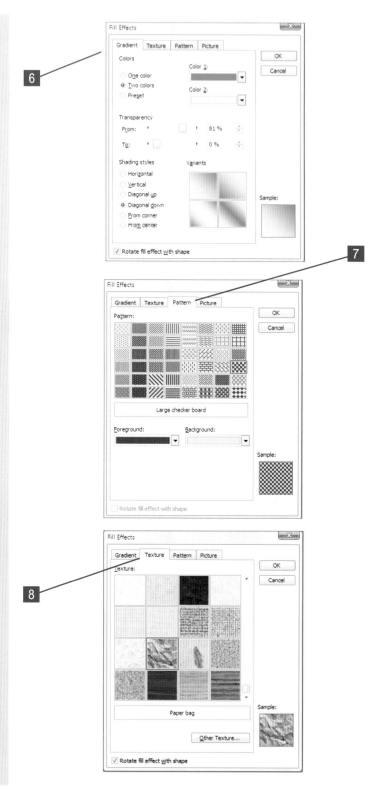

6 With a Gradient fill you can create a shaded background where one colour merges into another, or a single colour goes from dark to light, in a variety of patterns.

7 As well as patterned fills, you can also have patterned lines. Try them for distinctive frames – you can reach them from the Line Colour panel.

8 A Textured Fill Effect can give an interesting background to a box.

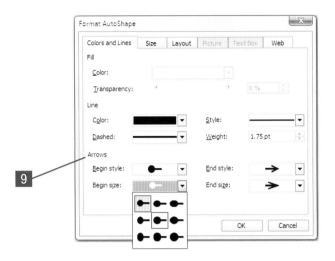

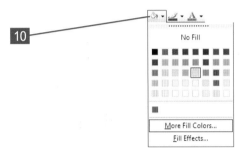

9 Add arrowheads from the Format dialogue box – double-click on a line to open this.

10 The drop-down palette has the basic colours, and access to the full palette (if you click on More Fill Colours…).

See also

The drawing tools used here belong to Microsoft Draw, a program that runs within Word (or any other Microsoft Office application). There's more about Microsoft Draw in Chapter 6.

5

Using columns

Word's layout facilities are almost as good as you will find in dedicated DTP (desktop publishing) software – its handling of columns is a good example.

You can set text in two or three columns, of the same or different widths, over the whole document or a selected part.

1 Select the text to set if only part is to be in columns.

2 Open the Format menu and select Columns...

3 Select the closest Preset design to set the number of columns.

4 Clear Equal column width and adjust the Width or Spacing if required.

5 Tick the Line between checkbox if a line is required.

6 Set the Apply to option.

7 Click OK.

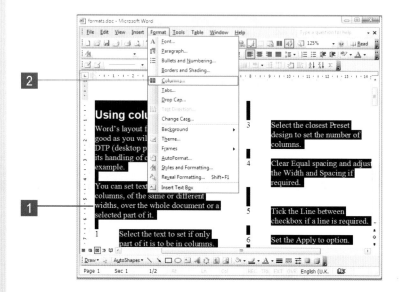

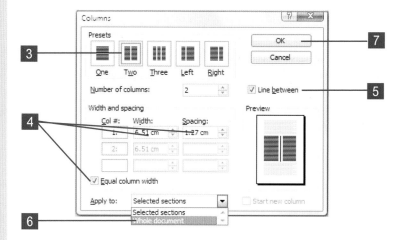

In a mail merge, a standard letter is combined with names and addresses from a data file to produce personalised letters or mailing labels. The data file can come from Access or another database system, or be created within Word. Its data is drawn into the Word document through merge fields, which link to fields in the data file.

Setting up a mail merge is straightforward, and is made even easier by the Mail Merge Wizard, which guides you through the process.

There are three stages:

- Create the main document – typically a standard letter or circular.
- Create the data source – which may mean typing the data into a new file, or locating an existing file.
- Merge the data into the document. There are three aspects to this:
  1. Inserting the merge fields into the document.
  2. Selecting the records to include from the data file.
  3. Outputting the merged letters.

The main document

This will have all its text, apart from the name and address, and perhaps other details of its recipients. It will be formatted and have its page setup and other options set, so that it is ready to run once the data has been added.

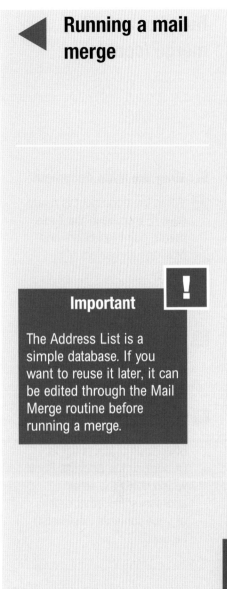

Running a mail merge

Important

The Address List is a simple database. If you want to reuse it later, it can be edited through the Mail Merge routine before running a merge.

5

Running a mail merge (cont.)

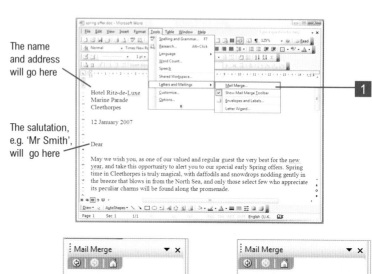

The name and address will go here

The salutation, e.g. 'Mr Smith', will go here

Creating the main document

1. When the document is ready, save it, then open the Tools menu, point to Letters and Mailings and select Mail Merge …

2. Select the document type and click Next.

3. Select the starting document – in this example, I am using the current document – then click Next.

4. If you were using an existing data file, it would be opened now. Your contacts list in Outlook or the Address Book, which holds the email addresses and other details of your contacts, could also be used.

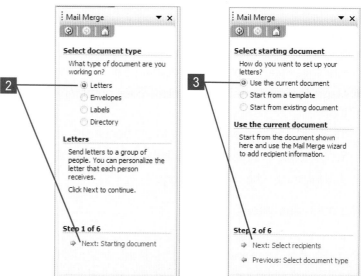

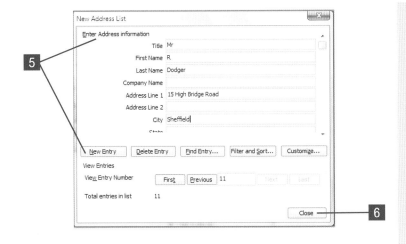

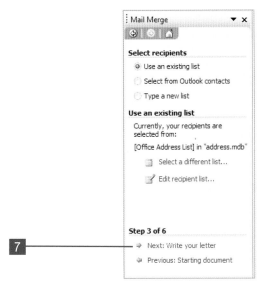

5 If you choose Type a new list, the New Address List dialogue box will open. Enter the address information for the recipients, clicking New Entry after each.

6 Click Close when you are done. You will be taken to the Save As dialogue box. Give a file name and select a folder to hold the file.

7 When you get back to the Wizard, click Next: Write your letter to move to the next step.

5

Running a mail merge (cont.)

If the letter has not yet been written, or it needs editing, the text can be typed now. This is also the time for bringing in information from the data source.

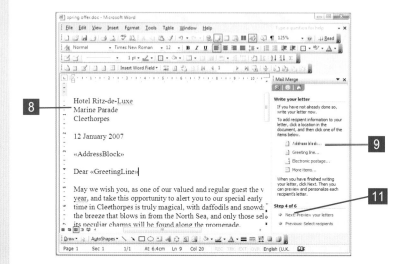

Incorporating data

8 Place the insertion point where you want the first field to be written.

9 Select the Address block, Greeting line or other item from the list in the Task pane.

10 A dialogue box will open. Set the options for the item as required and click OK.

11 Click Next to preview your letters.

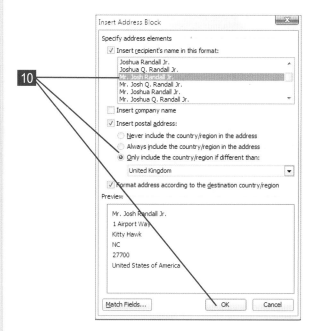

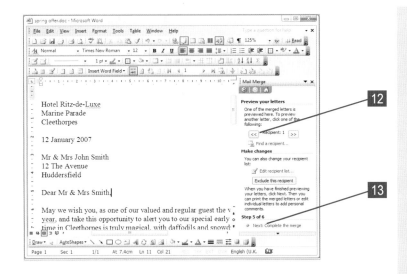

Running a mail merge (cont.)

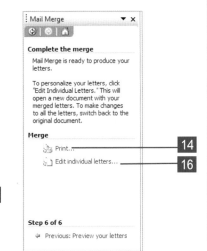

12 At the preview stage, check through enough of your letters to see how the merge will work. If the text or fields need to be edited, do that now.

13 Click Next to complete the merge.

14 If no further editing is required, click Print.

15 Select the records to print and click OK.

16 If you want to personalise the mailing, click Edit individual letters and edit selected merged letters as required before printing.

Did you know?

You can insert any items from your address list, e.g. the recipient's first name, into your letter. Click Move items at Step 2 and select from the Insert Merge fields dialogue box.

5

Graphics

Introduction

There are many graphics applications currently in use. They can be divided into two main categories according to the way images are created and stored: vector and bitmap.

With vector graphics, the image is defined by the size, angle, colour and other properties of the lines and shapes that make it up. These remain separate elements, and can be selected and edited at any time. Microsoft Draw is an example of a simple vector graphics application, and the subject of the first half of this chapter.

In bitmap graphics software, the screen is treated like an artist's canvas. When a line or shape or dot of colour is applied, it becomes part of the whole picture. You may be able to undo the last few changes, but beyond that you cannot select a line, shape or dot and move, resize or edit it. The picture is stored by recording the colour of each pixel (bit) of the screen (map). The Windows accessory Paint is an example of a simple bitmap graphics application.

As well as creating images directly on the computer using drawing and painting software, you can also bring in images from outside. In the last few years, storing and displaying photos from digital cameras has become a major use for home computers. We'll look at digital cameras and the PC in the latter half of this chapter.

What you'll do

Discover Microsoft Draw

Start a drawing

Draw lines

Use AutoShapes

Draw freehand

Rotate and flip

Add text to a drawing

Store digital photos

Use Photo Gallery

Adjust exposure

Adjust colour

Crop a picture

File from Photo Gallery

Email photos

Print photos

Discovering Microsoft Draw

Draw is a set of drawing tools that can be called up in any Microsoft Office application – it is not really a separate program.

It can be used in two separate ways:

- Elements can be drawn, as separate items, in amongst the ordinary text.
- You can create a Draw object within a document. If the object is moved or resized, then all the drawn elements inside it are moved and resized along with it.

To draw single elements, you only need to have the Drawing toolbar visible.

For the next few pages, we will be working in Draw objects. The drawing techniques are the same whether you are working with Draw objects or single elements.

To display the drawing toolbar

1. Right-click on any toolbar.

2. Click Drawing so that a tick appears beside it.

3. Use this approach when you want to add a line, arrow or other simple item to your text.

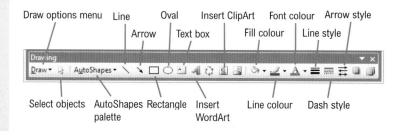

Important

The only way to learn to use these – or any – tools is to play with them. Experiment and enjoy!

When you start a new drawing, a 'canvas' is marked out on the screen and the AutoShapes and Drawing toolbars appear. If the canvas is the wrong size or in the wrong place, it can be resized at any time and moved into place when you have finished.

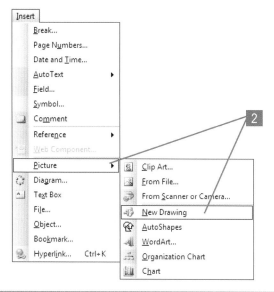

1 Click into the document where you want the drawing to go.

2 Open the Insert menu, point to Picture and select New Drawing. Wait a moment.

To draw simple rectangles or ovals

3 Click on the tool you want.

4 Click where you want one corner of the shape to be placed.

5 Drag to create the shape.

To end drawing and return to editing the document

6 Click anywhere on the document outside the drawing canvas.

To edit the drawing later

7 Double-click inside the drawing canvas.

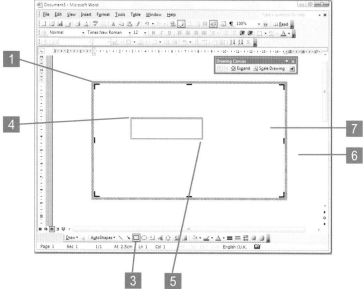

Timesaver tip

To produce a perfect square (or circle), hold down [Shift] while you draw a rectangle (or oval).

Drawing lines

Straight lines are drawn by clicking and dragging, but remember that once drawn they can easily be resized, moved or removed.

Arrows are drawn and formatted in the same way as a line. In fact, an arrow is simply a line with a head on one or both ends, so a line can be converted to or from and arrow.

To draw a line or arrow

1. Click on the line or arrow tool.
2. Click where you want one end of the line to be.
3. Drag to the required length.

To adjust a line or arrow

4. Click on the line to select it.
5. Drag on the middle of the line to move it.
6. Drag on a handle to change the angle or length.

To format a line or arrow

7. Select from the options on the drop-down lists from the Line Style, Dash Style and Arrow Style tools.

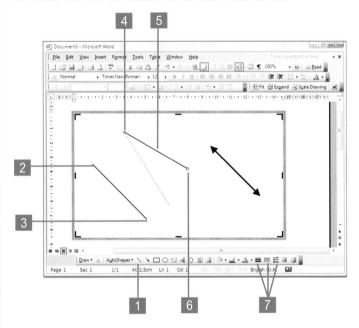

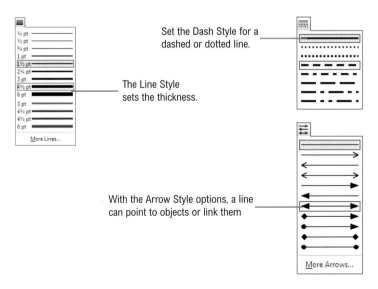

Set the Dash Style for a dashed or dotted line.

The Line Style sets the thickness.

With the Arrow Style options, a line can point to objects or link them

Simple regular shapes can be drawn from the toolbar buttons, as we saw earlier. But you are not limited to these. There are over 100 AutoShapes – patterns for a wide variety of shapes.

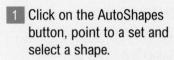

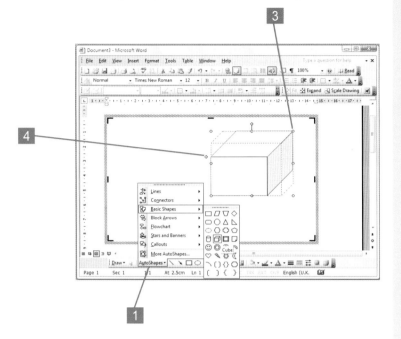

1 Click on the AutoShapes button, point to a set and select a shape.

or

2 On the AutoShapes toolbar, click on a set button and select a shape.

3 Click and drag to draw the shape.

4 If the shape has a yellow diamond, this is a handle that you can use to change its proportions, e.g. the height relative to length. Drag on the diamond to set the proportions.

Drawing freehand

You can draw shapes by hand, though drawing smooth lines with a mouse is very hard! If there are no suitable AutoShapes, you might want to give this a try.

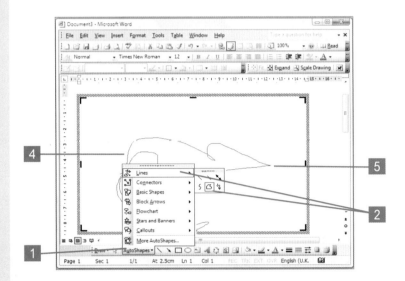

1 Click the AutoShapes button on the Drawing toolbar.

2 Select the Lines set, and select Freeform.

or

3 Click on the first button on the AutoShapes toolbar, and select Freeform.

4 Click to start the shape, then drag to draw.

5 Double-click when you have finished – if the start and end do not meet and you then fill the shape, Draw will treat them as if they were joined by a straight line.

Timesaver tip

If you want to use any tool several times, double-click on it at the start. It will then stay selected until you choose another tool.

The menu that opens from the Draw button holds options for manipulating objects, including the Rotate or Flip set.

Flip

You can flip an object in either of two ways:

- Flip Horizontal – reflects it as if it were standing next to a mirror
- Flip Vertical – reflects it as if it were standing on top of a mirror.

Apart from Free Rotate, these all work by first selecting the object then giving the command.

To flip an object

1 Select the object.

2 Click the Draw button and point to Rotate or Flip.

3 Select a Rotate or Flip option.

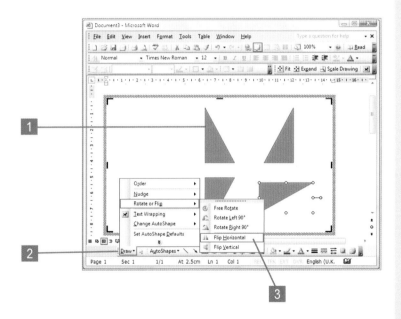

Timesaver tip

To copy a shape, select it and click Copy, then click Paste and drag the new shape into position.

Rotating and flipping (cont.)

4 Select the object.

To rotate by 90°

5 Click the Draw button, point to Rotate or Flip and select Rotate Left or Right.

To use Free Rotate

6 Select the Free Rotate option.

7 Drag on one of the green handles to pull the object round – a dotted outline will show you how it will look.

8 Click on the background to turn off the rotate handles.

Rotate

There are three ways to rotate an object:

- Free Rotate – allows you to rotate the object by any amount around its centre
- Rotate Left – rotates it 90° anticlockwise
- Rotate Right – rotates it 90° clockwise.

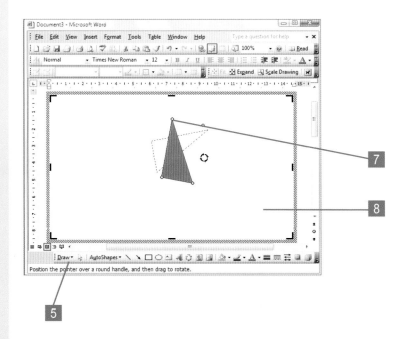

Drawn objects can be placed directly amongst text, as we saw earlier, but this is not the best way to combine text and drawings.

With a text box, you can place your text exactly where you want it in the drawing.

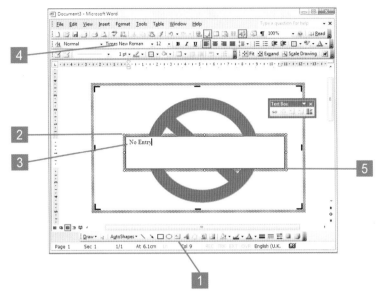

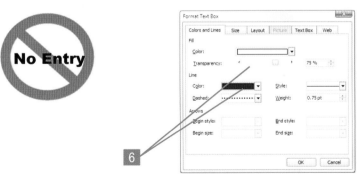

Adding text to a drawing

6

1 Select the Text Box tool .

2 Click at one corner of where you want the box and drag to the opposite corner.

3 Type your text.

4 Select the text and format it as usual, using the tools on the Formatting toolbar and the options on the Format menu.

5 If you want to move or resize the text box, click on an edge to select the box rather than its text, then drag on a frame or handle to move or resize the object.

6 By default the text box will have a thin black outline, but not be filled. To format the line (set it to No Colour to turn it off) or set the Fill Colour or transparency, right-click on the box and select Format Text Box, then use the options in the dialogue box.

Storing digital photos

It is so simple to copy or move photos from your digital camera onto your Vista PC. Vista treats the memory card in the camera as if it were a removable hard drive or CD – all you need to do is connect them together. You can do this in two ways: either use a cable to link a USB port on the PC with the USB port on your camera, or take the memory card out of the camera and plug it directly into the matching card slot on your PC. (Not all PCs have these.)

1 Link the camera and the PC with a USB cable, and turn the camera on, in display mode.

or

2 Take the memory card out of the camera and plug it into a matching port on the PC.

3 A new Explorer window will open, showing the top level folder on the camera's memory. Open the folders down to the one holding the photos.

4 You must be able to see the folder you want to store the pictures in and the one on the camera. Adjust the Folders list display to bring the target folder into view, or open a new Explorer window and open the target folder in that.

5 Select the photo(s) you want to transfer to your PC.

To copy photos, leaving them in the camera memory

6 Drag the selected photos across into the target folder.

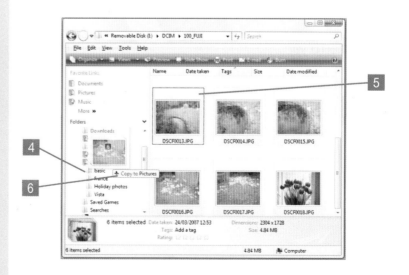

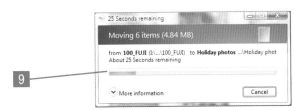

| Copy Here |
| Move Here | 8
| Create Shortcuts Here |
| Cancel |

25 Seconds remaining

Moving 6 items (4.84 MB)

from **100_FUJI** (I:\...\100_FUJI) to **Holiday photos** ...\Holiday phot
About 25 Seconds remaining

9

⌄ More information   Cancel

To move photos from the camera memory onto the hard drive

7 Hold down the right mouse button and drag the selected photos to the target folder.

8 Release the mouse button. A menu will appear – select Move Here.

9 Wait while the photos are transferred.

!

Important

Your camera will have come with its own image management and editing software. This may be very good and have special features all of its own, but for most purposes you may find it is simplest to manage your photos with Explorer and the Photo Gallery (see next page).

Using Photo Gallery

The Windows Photo Gallery is part of the Vista package of programs and accessories. It may be called 'gallery' but this is far more than just a viewer for your photos. You can use it to copy, delete, print, email, or edit any picture file.

Once you have opened the gallery for one file, you can use it to work through the other images in the same folder.

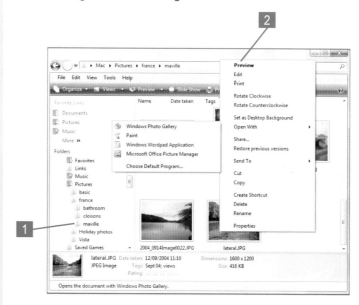

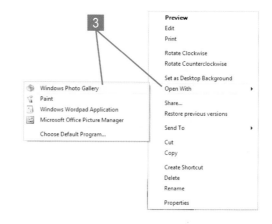

1. In Windows Explorer, open the folder that contains the pictures you want to view or edit.

2. Double-click on a photo to select it, or right-click on it, and select Preview.

3. If a different application opens, close it, then right-click on the photo, point to Open With and select Photo Gallery.

4. When the Photo Gallery opens, explore its tools.

Important

Double-clicking on an image or using the Preview command will open the linked application for the image type. By default this will be Photo Gallery, but it may have been replaced by the camera's own editing software, or another application.

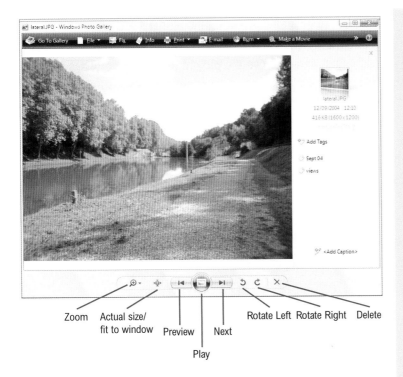

Zoom   Actual size/   Rotate Left   Rotate Right   Delete
         fit to window   Preview   Next

                        Play

Did you know?

You can add tags or a caption to files in the Photo
Gallery. Just click in the Add Tags or Add Caption fields
and type your text.

Adjusting the exposure

The beauty of digital photography is that, unlike film-based photography, the picture you see is not the final image. You can adjust and improve the picture in a variety of ways – and you don't need a darkroom to change the exposure or the colour balance.

1. Click Fix on the toolbar above the picture.

2. Click Adjust Exposure in the sidebar on the right. A small panel will open below.

3. Drag the Brightness and Colour sliders to adjust the levels.

4. If you do not like the changes you have made, click Undo to go back.

5. If you have moved on to another picture, and then returned to an adjusted one, you can still undo the changes, but you will be asked if you want to revert to the original version. Click Revert to do so.

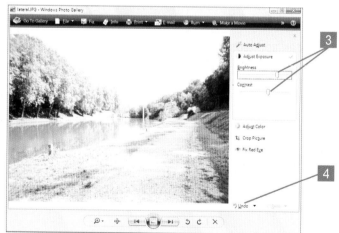

In digital photographs, as in any kind of computer images, colours are produced by mixing red, blue and green light. By varying the combinations and intensity, the full range of hues and shades can be generated. Photo Gallery gives you three ways to adjust colours:

- Colour temperature controls the amount of blue in the image – a high level of blue makes it look cold!

- Tint controls the green red balance.

- Saturation controls the overall amount of colour, on a scale which goes from pure greys to very vibrant colours.

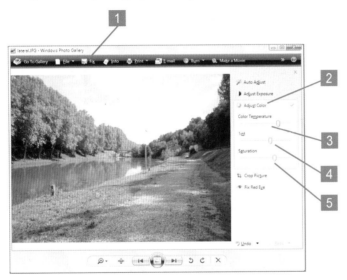

Adjusting the colour

6

To adjust the colour balance

1 If the editing sidebar is not already open, click Fix.

2 Click Adjust Colour to open its panel.

3 Drag Colour Temperature to the left to increase the level of blue.

4 Drag the Tint slider to the left to increase the green level, or right for a redder image.

5 Drag the Saturation slider to the left to make the picture greyer, or to the right for richer colours.

Timesaver tip

Nudge all the sliders to the right to give outdoor shots a sun-drenched feel.

Cropping a picture

1. If the editing sidebar is not already open, click Fix.

2. Click Crop Picture to open the cropping panel.

3. Open the Proportion drop-down list.

4. Select the size that you want to use for printing, or otherwise outputting the image.

5. Click Rotate Frame if you need to switch from landscape to portrait layout, or vice versa.

6. A bright rectangle indicates the area to be retained after cropping. Drag the corners of the outline to change the cropped size.

7. Click anywhere within the rectangle and drag to move the crop area.

8. When you are happy with the selection, click Apply.

It often seems to be more difficult to frame a photo accurately with a digital camera than with a traditional one. The screens can be hard to see on sunny days, and the viewfinders – if present – are rarely good guides. But it's not a major problem because you can easily crop a photo to remove unwanted material from around the central image.

Cropping is also useful before printing a picture. If you ensure that the image has the same proportions as the paper, then – though it may be shrunk or expanded to fit – it will not be distorted in the printed image.

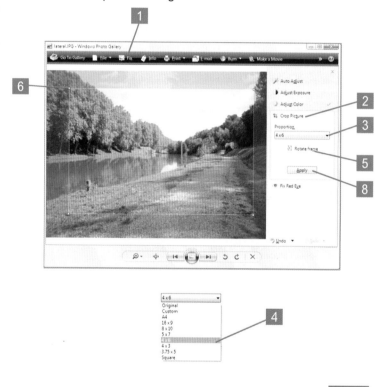

Important

Don't forget that if you get the crop wrong, the Undo button will restore your original.

You can use Photo Gallery to perform the usual filing jobs, like deleting, coping and renaming, but you can also do more. For a start, there are two copying operations.

The Copy command copies the image to the Windows Clipboard so that it can be pasted into another application.

Make a copy copies the file either into another folder and/or with a different name. It will still be the same type – if you want to save the file as a different type, you need to open it in Paint or another graphics program.

There is also a Revert to Original option here, which can be very handy if your adjusting and cropping efforts have not gone as well as you had hoped.

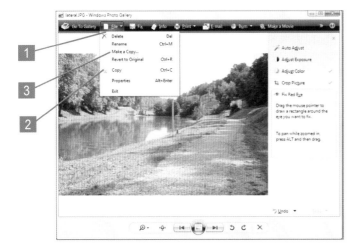

To copy a file

1. Click the File button to open its menu.

2. To copy to the Clipboard, so that you can paste it elsewhere, select Copy.

   or

3. Select Make a Copy… to open the Make a Copy dialogue box.

4. If you want to keep the copy in the same folder (or if you just want to change the name anyway), edit the File name.

5. If you want to save it in a different folder, type the path, or select it from the drop-down list at the top, or click Browse folders and select the folder there.

6. Click Save.

Emailing photos

The average digital camera can take photos with a resolution of 4 megapixels or more, and you need this high resolution for good quality printing. However, most computer screens are only 1240 by 1028 pixels – around 1 megapixel. If you are sending someone a photo to view on their screen you may as well reduce it down to a sensible size first. It will get there faster, and take up less space in their inbox or hard drive.

If you email the photo directly from Photo Gallery, you can use the built-in routine to reduce the image size before you send it.

1 Click the Email button on the toolbar.

2 Select a Picture Size.

3 Click Attach. There will be a delay while the image is processed and your email software activated.

4 A new message window will open with the photo attached, and the Subject line filled in. Select the recipient and add your own message.

5 Click Send.

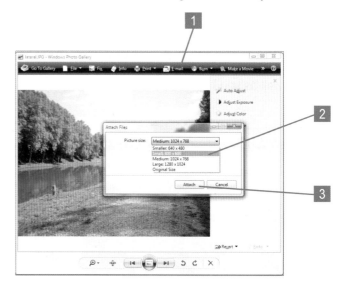

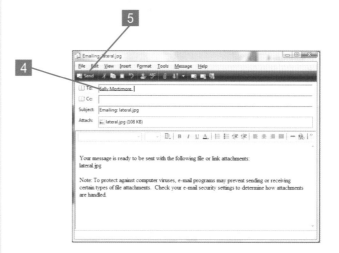

166

Photo Gallery has a print routine that will print one or more photos at a time, on a range of paper sizes, with a variety of layouts. If you want to print more than one photo – as distinct from several copies of the same photo – you must first switch to the Gallery's alternative display, where you can select multiple pictures.

To print several photos at once

1. Make sure your printer is loaded with the right type of paper.

2. Click the Go To Gallery button on the toolbar.

3. In the Explorer-style display, select the photos you want to print.

4. Click the Print button and select Print...

Printing photos (cont.)

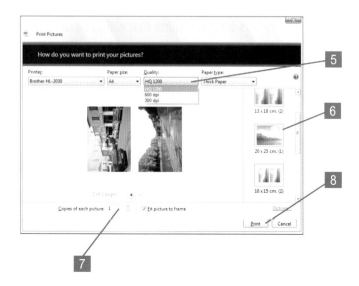

5 At the Print Pictures window, select the Printer, Paper size, Quality and Paper type.

6 Pick a layout from the list on the right.

7 If you want more than one copy of each picture, set the number.

8 Click Print.

Timesaver tip

If you only want to print one photo, start the Print routine from the normal, single-image display, and continue from step 4.

More about Windows

7

Introduction

In this chapter we will go a little deeper into Windows. None of this is essential for the day-to-day running of your PC, and I know of quite a few long-time PC users who have never got round to exploring any of the features covered here – and never missed it. I think they are missing out. The more you understand about the possibilities of your PC, the more you can do, and the easier you can do things. Most of the things dealt with in this chapter are ways to adapt the Windows environment so that it is easier for you to work with. Read on and find out how to change the appearance of the screen – perhaps to make it more accessible, or simply to make it look the way you like it; tailor the mouse to your touch; organise the Start menu, Task bar and the Desktop; set up the PC for multiple users; and add gadgets to your Desktop.

Exploring the Control Panel

The Control Panel lets you customise some aspects of Windows to your own tastes.

Some settings are best left at the defaults; some should be set when new hardware or software is added to the system; some should be set once then left alone; a few can be adjusted at any time.

What is in your Control panel depends upon the hardware and software on your system. Open yours to see what is there.

1. Click the Start button.

2. Select Control Panel.

3. The Control Panel has two alternative display modes. The default view groups the controls according to what they do. This is probably the best for new users. Click on a link to see the next level.

4. At the second level of the Control Panel, you can pick a task or an icon to adjust a setting.

5. Click the Back button to return to the top level.

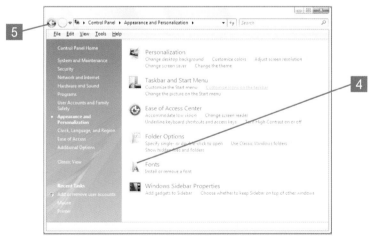

Exploring the Control Panel (cont.)

6 The Control Panel can also be run in Classic view. This gives direct access to the Control Panel icons. Click the Classic view link in the left-hand panel.

7 If you want to switch back to the default view, click Control Panel Home in the sidebar.

Setting the Date and Time

The date and time can be adjusted if you want, though this should rarely be necessary. You can get Windows to handle Summer Time changes for you, and even get it to keep the clock accurate automatically.

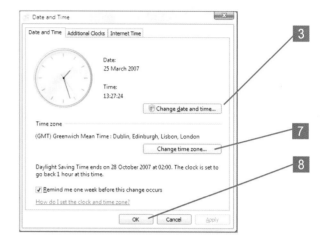

1 In the Control Panel click the Clock, Language and Region link.

2 Select Date and Time.

3 On the Date & Time tab, click Change Date and Time.

4 Use the Calendar to set the date.

5 Select the hour and minute figures in turn and type in the correct value.

6 Click on OK.

7 Click Change Time Zone and use the drop-down list if it needs changing.

8 Click OK to close and save your changes.

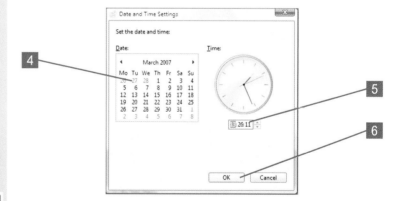

Did you know?

You can have several clocks if you need to know the time in different time zones. Set them up on the Additional Clocks tab.

Timesaver tip

On the Internet Time tab you can turn on an option to synchronise the clock with an Internet time server. It will then check the time once a week automatically. If you are online regularly, this is well worth doing.

Windows display options are not just decorative. If you spend a lot of time in front of your screen, it is important that you can see it clearly and use it comfortably.

A theme sets the overall style for the Desktop – its background image, the icons for the standard Windows tools, the colours and fonts, and the sounds that are triggered by alerts and prompts. If there are parts of the theme that you don't like, you can modify them on the other tabs. If you are used to earlier versions of Windows you can switch to the Classic display.

Customising the display

Selecting a theme

7

1. Start from Appearance and Personalisation and select Change the theme.

2. Open the Themes drop-down list, and select a theme. It will be previewed in the Sample pane.

3. Click .

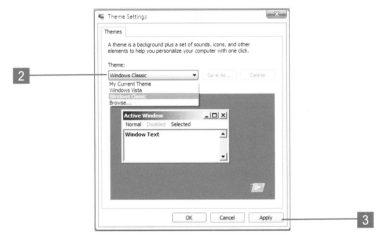

Timesaver tip

If you modify a theme, click Save As and save it with a new name. If you ever change the theme, you can then easily restore your carefully modified one.

Themes have an impact on every part of the display.

Customising the display (cont.)

Choosing a Wallpaper

1. At the Control Panel, select Appearance and Personalisation, then Change desktop background.

2. Select a Picture Location from the drop-down list – Windows Wallpapers has a good set of suitable images.

   or

3. Click Browse and find the folder that contains the image you want to use.

4. Select the image.

5. Choose how you want the picture to be positioned – if it is not big enough to fill the screen, it can be stretched to fit, or tiled as a pattern.

6. Click OK to apply the choice.

7. Click the Back button to return to the Personalisation options.

The Desktop

The Wallpaper is the background to the Desktop. There is a set of designs to choose from, or you can use any image (in .BMP, .GIF or .JPG format) or a web page.

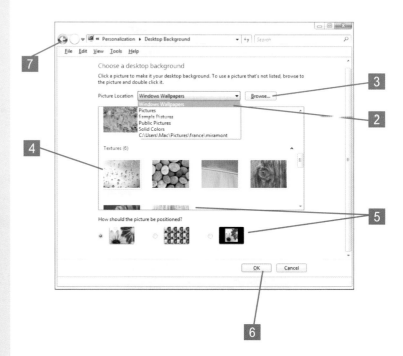

See also

There's more about tidying the Desktop on page 193.

The colour selection that you make here will be applied to the windows, the Task bar and the Start menu. You can choose from preset colours, or mix your own.

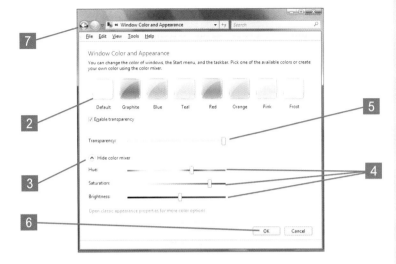

Using colours

1 At the Control Panel, select Appearance and Personalisation, then Customise colours.

2 Pick a colour.

or

3 Click Show colour mixer (its label will then change to Hide colour mixer).

4 Use the sliders to set the hue, saturation and brightness.

5 Set the Transparency level – move the slider to the left to increase transparency.

6 Click OK to apply the choice.

7 Click the Back button to return to the Personalisation options.

7

Customising the display (cont.)

Setting a screen saver

1. At the Control Panel select Appearance and Personalisation, then Change screen saver.

2. Select a screen saver from the drop-down list and click Preview to run it on screen.

3. Click Settings and set the options to suit yourself.

4. For password protection, turn on the option On resume, display logon screen.

5. Click [Apply] to apply your choices but keep the dialogue box open.

A screen saver switches to a moving image after the system has been inactive for a few minutes. These were useful on old monitors, as static images could burn into the screen if left on too long. This is not a problem with new monitors, but screen savers still have their uses. If you set it to be password protected, once the screen saver has started, it can only be turned off by entering the password – so you can leave your desk knowing that your work will be safe from passers-by once the screen saver starts up.

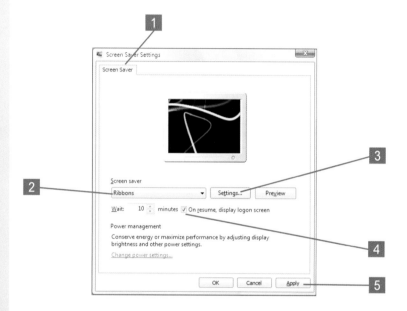

The Photos option in the screen savers gives you a constantly changing display of images. It's ideal for running a slide show of your favourite photos. These can be collected into a single folder, or marked by a special tag.

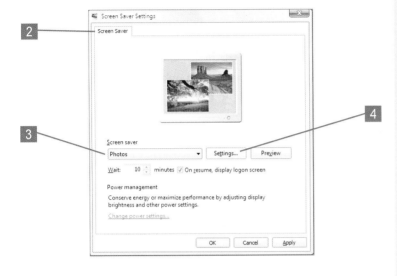

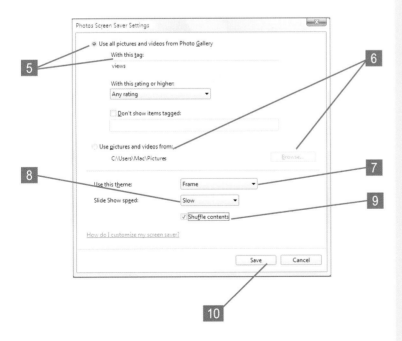

Slide show screen savers

1 Locate your favourite photos or other images and move or copy them into one folder.

2 Go to the Screen saver routine in the Control Panel.

3 Select Photos as the screen saver.

4 Click Settings to open the Photo Screen Saver Settings dialogue box.

5 Select Use all pictures from the Photo Gallery, and specify the selection with a tag.

or

6 Click Use pictures and videos from and set the folder to use.

7 Specify the theme – this sets the style of the display and of the transitions between slides.

8 Set the speed.

9 Turn on Shuffle contents to randomise the order.

10 Click Save to save the settings and return to the screen saver tab.

Defining the
screen settings

The Display settings control the resolution and colours of the monitor screen. Finding the right resolution for you is a matter of the balance between quality and quantity – more pixels give you larger windows but smaller type. Higher Colours settings produce a prettier screen but take more memory and time to update. Find the levels that you can work best with.

Do not change the Advanced options unless the current display is not working properly *and* you know what you are doing. You can switch to a display mode that is not properly supported by your hardware, resulting in a screen which is impossible to read – and therefore impossible to correct!

1 On the Control Panel select Appearance and Personalisation, then Adjust screen resolution.

2 Adjust the Resolution – try it at the highest setting first. If you do not like this, try the next one down until you reach the right level for you.

3 Set the Colour quality level. Again, start at the highest setting, and only switch to a lower one if you find that this seems to slow down the system.

4 Click Apply – the new settings will be applied.

5 A dialogue box will appear asking if you want to keep the new settings. Click No at the prompt to go back to the original ones.

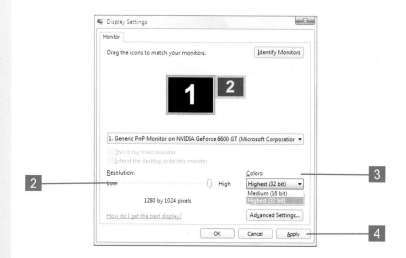

Work in Windows is much easier if you are comfortable with your mouse. Use the Mouse Properties panel to set the way that it responds.

Don't change to Left-handed unless you are the only one who uses the PC, and it is the only system that you ever use. Ideally, you should learn to use the mouse with either hand.

- The Double-Click Speed sets the difference between a double-click and two separate clicks.
- Pointer Speed links speed and distance, so that the faster you move the mouse, the further the pointer goes.

Find speeds that suit you and stick with them. If you keep changing them, you will never get the feel of the mouse.

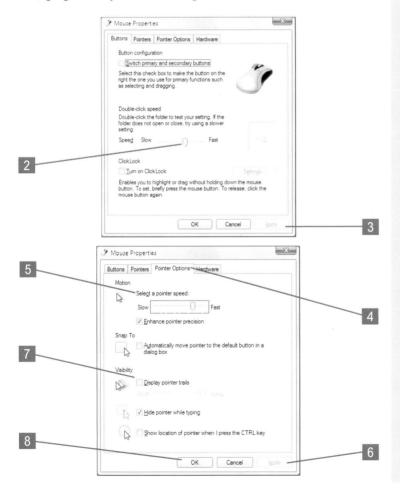

Controlling the mouse

1. Open the Control Panel. Under Hardware and Sound, select Mouse.
2. On the Buttons panel, set the Double-click speed and double-click in the Test area to see if the system responds.
3. Click Apply.
4. Go to the Pointer Options panel.
5. Set the Pointer Speed.
6. Click Apply to test the new speed setting.
7. Turn on the Pointer trails and set the size.
8. Click OK to close and keep your settings.

?

Did you know?

A pointer trail makes the mouse easier to see on LCD screens.

Attaching sounds to events

Windows allows you to attach sounds to events. These can be seen as useful ways of alerting you to what's happening or as more modern noise pollution. It all depends upon your point of view. I like a fanfare when the system is ready to start work (to wake me up – well, you wait so long!) but few other sounds. Try them out – the Utopia sounds are worth listening to.

The other tabs can be used to change the Audio and Voice devices or fine-tune their volume controls. The devices are best left to the system. The volume controls can be reached more simply from the icon on the Taskbar.

1 At the Control Panel select Hardware and Sound, then Change system sounds.

2 Open the Sounds tab.

3 Pick a Scheme.

4 Select an event.

5 Click `▶ Test` to preview its sound.

6 Sample a few more and go back to Step 3 and try alternative schemes until you find one you prefer.

7 To set individual sounds, select the event then pick a new sound from the Sounds list or Browse for an alternative.

8 Click `Apply` or `OK`.

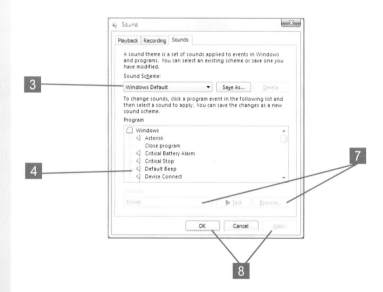

Important

You can use the Test hardware and Troubleshoot routines on the Audio, Voice and Hardware tabs if you have problems with the sound systems.

The volume can be controlled in several ways. The simplest, of course, is to use the knob on your speakers, or if you are too lazy to reach across the desk, you can use the volume control on the Task bar.

You can also set the volume separately for each application that produces sound, e.g. you could set the system sounds that alert you to errors, incoming mail and the like, to a lower level so that they don't interrupt the CD that you are listening to.

You can also configure the system to match your speaker setup.

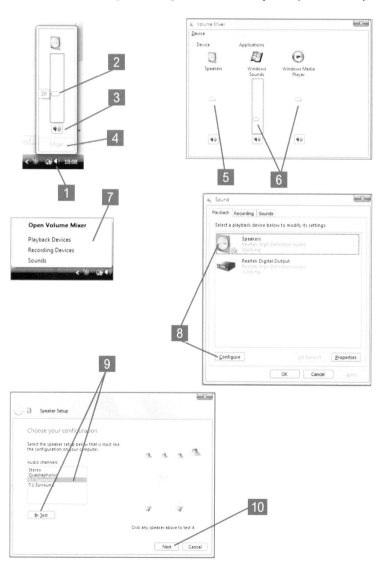

1 Click the Volume Control icon 🔊 on the right of the Task bar.

2 Drag the slider up or down as required.

or

3 Click the Mute icon 🔊 to turn the sounds off completely (or back on again).

To adjust the volume mix

4 On the volume control, click Mixer.

5 Set the overall volume for the device.

6 Set the level for each application that you have running.

To set up your speakers

7 Right-click on the Volume Control icon and select Playback Devices.

8 At the Sounds dialogue box, select the device and click Configure.

9 Choose your configuration, and click Test to check it.

10 Click Next to customise the setup, then Finish.

Setting Regional options

The Regional and Language Options control the units of measurement and the styles used by applications for displaying dates, time, currency and other numbers. The choice of region sets the basic formats, but any or all of these can be customised.

1. Start from Clock, Language and Region in the Control Panel and click Regional and Language Options.

2. On the Formats tab select the country.

To customise the settings

3. Click [Customize this format...].

4. Work through the tabs.

5. To change any aspect, pick from its drop-down list.

6. Click [OK].

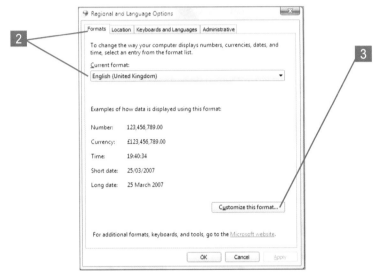

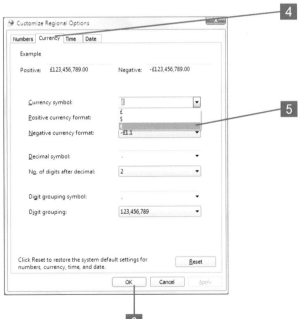

Timesaver tip

The Date and Time can be set more easily through the Clock – see page 172.

The Keyboards and Languages tab lets you enter foreign language text using the keyboard. This changes the letters produced by the keys and is best suited to touch-typists who are used to a foreign keyboard. Most of us are better off selecting foreign characters from the Character Map.

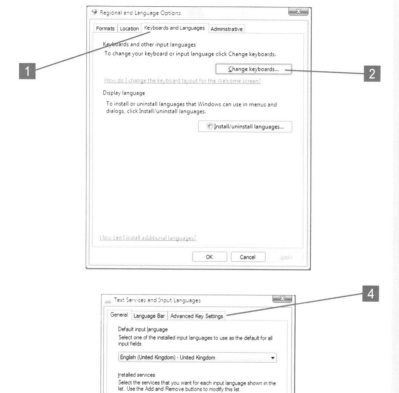

7

Adding other languages

1 In the Regional and Language Options dialogue box, switch to the Keyboards and Languages tab.

2 Click [Change keyboards...].

3 At the Text Services and Input Languages box, click Add and then pick the language.

4 To define a shortcut for switching the keyboard, use the Advanced Key Settings tab.

5 Click [OK].

For your information

If you have other languages installed on your PC and want to use them in your dialogue boxes and menus, click the Install/uninstall languages... button and follow the instructions. If you would like to install other languages, go to the Microsoft website and search for 'Language Interface Pack'. There are lots available for free download.

Improving accessibility

Windows offer a range of ways to make life easier for people with sight, hearing or motor control disabilities – though the keyboard alternative to the mouse may well be useful to other people as well.

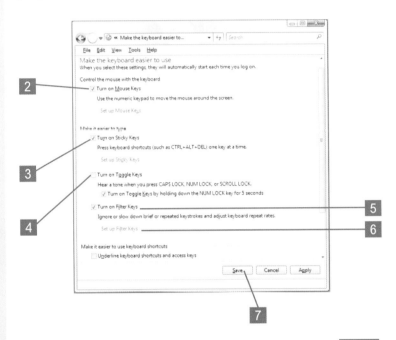

Using the Keyboard

1. On the Control Panel, select Ease of Access, and then click Change how your keyboard works.

2. Turn on Mouse Keys to use the number pad as a control for the mouse pointer.

3. Turn on Sticky Keys if you want to be able to type [Ctrl], [Shift] and [Alt] combinations by pressing one key at a time, rather than all at once.

4. Turn on Toggle Keys if you want to be alerted by a sounds when any of the Lock keys are pressed.

5. Turn on Filter Keys if you find that keystrokes are sometimes repeated because you type very slowly.

6. Click the Set up link in any of these areas to fine tune the settings.

7. Click Save.

Important

You can replace the sounds that Windows uses to alert you to events with visible alerts, using the options on the Sound tab of this dialogue box.

You can also make the mouse easier to see, or replace it with keystrokes. If the Mouse Keys option is turned on, the arrow keys on the Number pad can be used to move the mouse pointer, and the central key [5] acts as the left mouse button. Movement is more limited than an actual mouse – you can only move up, down, left or right and not diagonally – but it is easier to control.

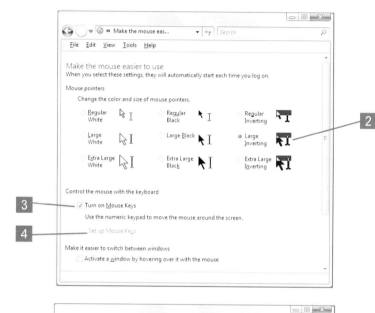

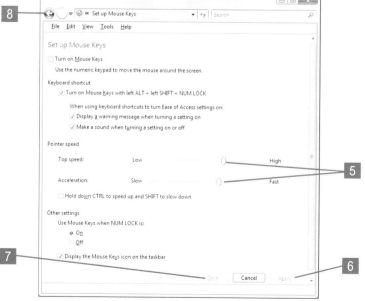

Setting up Mouse Keys

1. At the Ease of Access Centre, select Change how your mouse works.

2. Set the size and colour of the mouse pointer.

3. Tick the checkbox to turn on Mouse Keys.

4. Click the Set up Mouse Keys link to adjust the key settings.

5. Experiment with the Speed and Acceleration settings to find the most workable levels.

6. If you click Apply, the settings will be activated without you leaving this window.

7. When you are happy with the settings, click Save.

8. Click the Back button to return to the Ease of Access Centre.

Improving accessibility (cont.)

To use a high contrast display

1. In the Ease of Access Centre, select Optimise visual display.

2. Click Choose a High Contrast colour scheme.

3. At the dialogue box, select a scheme and click OK.

4. If you want to be able to switch between high contrast and normal, tick the Turn on or off High Contrast checkbox, then set its options.

5. For audio assistance, turn on the Narrator and/or Audio Description options.

To improve visibility

6. Click Change the size of text and icons. At the Scaling dialogue box, set the new scale and click OK.

7. Turn on the Magnifier.

8. Scroll down the window and explore the other options. Making the cursor thicker and setting a slower blink rate can make it easier to see.

9. Click Save when you have finished.

Optimising the display

There are several ways to make the screen easier to read. A high contrast colour scheme is the most obvious of these. Others include the Narrator, which will read any text on the screen, the Magnifier which zooms in on the area under the cursor, and changing the size and blink rate of the cursor.

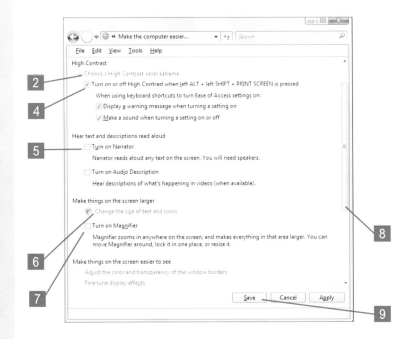

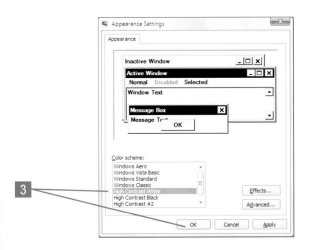

The Start menu can be customised in several ways. You can very easily change its appearance and control which items are shown in the main display. With just a little more effort, you can also reorganise shortcuts in the All Programs area, adding, moving or removing them as required.

The most dramatic change you can make is to switch to the Classic Start menu. This could be a good move if you have used and are comfortable with an earlier version of Windows. The Classic Start menu is neater, but lacks the quick links to your main applications. It can be customised in the same way as in earlier versions of Windows, with routines for adding and removing menu items.

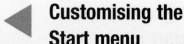

7

1 Right-click on the Start button and select Properties.

2 Select the menu style.

3 Clear the checkboxes for Store and display... if you don't want other people to know what you are working on.

4 Click [OK].

Important !

If you are one of several users on a PC, remember that every user has his or her own Start menu, so feel free to customise yours to suit yourself.

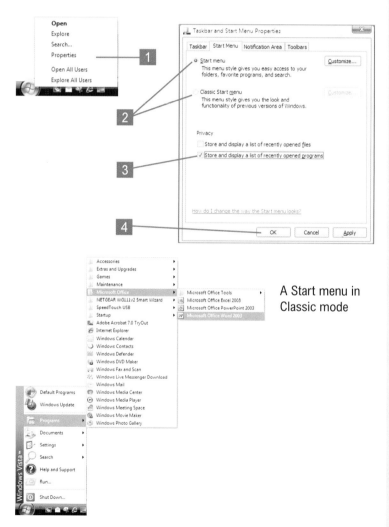

A Start menu in Classic mode

Customising the Start menu (cont.)

The Vista Start menu

1. Open the Start menu properties dialogue box.

2. Work through the main list of options, setting how – or if – you want standard items to be displayed.

3. Set the number of recent programs to show on the menu.

4. Your Web browser and email application are normally included in the Start menu. If you have alternatives to the standard Internet Explorer and Windows Mail, select them.

5. Click OK.

Not surprisingly, there are different sets of customising options for the standard Vista Start menu and the Classic Start menu.

On the Vista Start menu, the standard items, such as Computer, Documents and Games can be displayed as a menu, a link to a window – or not at all. The Vista system notes which programs you use most often, and includes these in the Start menu. You can set how many to include.

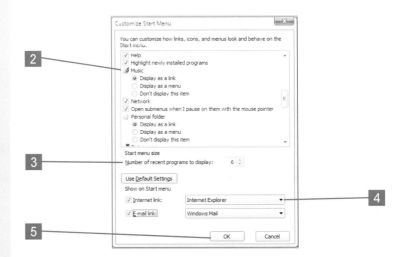

On the Classic Start menu you can control – to some extent – which programs are displayed in the All Programs menu, and adjust how they are displayed. The limitation is that the core of the menu is set by the system and cannot be changed by users.

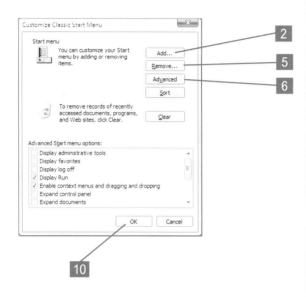

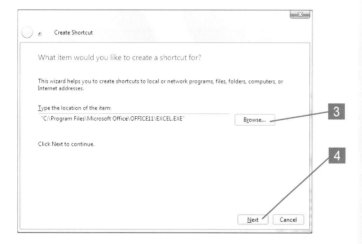

The Classic Start menu

1 Open the Start menu properties dialogue box.

To add a shortcut to a program

2 Click Add if you have a program that you would like to add to the menu – most have a menu entry created automatically when they are installed.

3 At the Create Shortcut window, Browse for the program – it will probably be somewhere in the Program Files folder.

4 Click Next. You can then edit the entry's name and decide which menu to put it in.

To remove an entry

5 Click Remove, select the entry and click Remove.

Customising the Start menu (cont.)

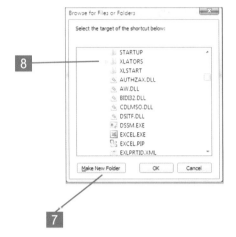

To change the menu

6 Click Advanced to open Explorer at the Programs folder. This is where shortcuts are stored.

7 If you want to set up a new menu, create a folder.

8 Drag shortcuts across into folders to move them in the menus.

9 Close the window when you have finished.

10 Click OK to save your changes.

A shortcut on the Desktop can be a convenient way of running a program that you use regularly. When new programs are installed, you are sometimes given the option of adding a Desktop shortcut. If not, or you decide later that you want one, you can set up a shortcut in a minute – and if you don't make much use of it, you can remove it even faster!

Sometimes when installing shareware or freeware programs downloaded from the web, Start menu or Desktop shortcuts are not created automatically, and you will have to do it yourself. It's not difficult.

1　Open the Start menu and find the program's entry.

2　Right-click on the entry and select Copy.

or

3　Right-click anywhere on the Desktop and select Paste Shortcut.

or

4　In Explorer, find the program file – it will have an EXE extension.

5　Right-click on the file and select Send To, Desktop from its context menu.

6　Edit the name – it will be 'Shortcut to...'.

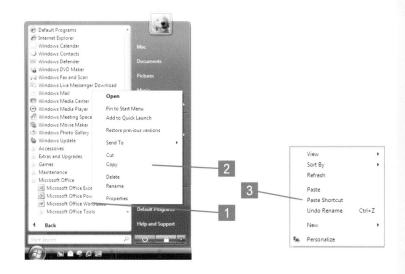

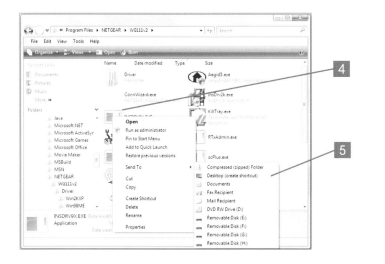

Timesaver tip

You can also create desktop shortcuts to files or folders, so that you can open them with a single click. Just right-click on them in Explorer and select Send To, Desktop.

Creating Desktop shortcuts (cont.)

Jargon buster

Shareware program – a program supplied on a try-before-you-buy basis. At the end of the trial period, you can continue to use the program for a small fee, typically £10 to £20. Shareware programs include the excellent WinZIP file compression software, and Paint Shop Pro, a fully-equipped image editing and creation package.

Jargon buster

Freeware – software ranging from well-meaning efforts of amateurs through to highly professional products like Acrobat Reader and Flash Player, which is given away so that people can view the documents and files created by paid-for applications. See pages 248–250 in Chapter 9 for more on these.

The Desktop can get cluttered with all these shortcuts, but it's simple enough to tidy it up. You can change the icon sizes, arrange them in different ways and turn them off altogether if you want a clear Desktop for any reason.

If you don't expect to ever use a shortcut again, select it and press [Delete]. Note that this only removes the shortcut, not the program, file or folder.

1 Right-click anywhere on the Desktop, point to View and select the icon size.

2 Right-click and point to View again, then tick Align to Grid to have the icons arranged in neat lines, and tick Auto Arrange if you want the system to tidy them up.

3 Right-click and point to Sort by.

4 Select the property that you want to sort by.

To hide the icons

5 Right-click and point to View, then clear the tick by Show Desktop Items.

Customising the Taskbar

Many parts of the Windows Vista system can be tailored to your own tastes. Some of the most important are covered in the next two chapters. We'll start with the Taskbar and the Start menu. You can adjust the size of the menu icons, turn the clock on or off, hide the Taskbar, or place it on any edge of the screen.

1 Right-click on any blank area of the Taskbar.

2 Select Properties from the context menu.

3 Set the options. Keep the taskbar on top – when off, to see the Taskbar you must minimise applications or press [Ctrl]-[Esc].

4 Auto-hide slides the Taskbar off-screen when not in use. Point off-screen to restore the Taskbar to view.

5 Group similar taskbar buttons – if the same program is running in several windows, they can all be stacked onto one button to save space.

6 Click [Apply] to see how they look.

7 Click [OK] to fix the settings and close.

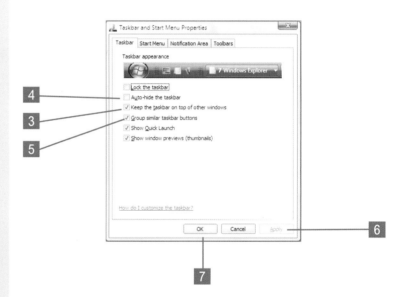

Moving the Taskbar is quite easy to do by mistake, so it is just as well to know how to do it intentionally – if only to correct a mistake!

Resizing the Taskbar – making it deeper or wider – is sometimes useful. Narrow vertical displays are almost unreadable. When you are running a lot of programs with a horizontal Taskbar, the titles on the buttons can be very small. If you deepen the display, you get two rows of decent-sized buttons.

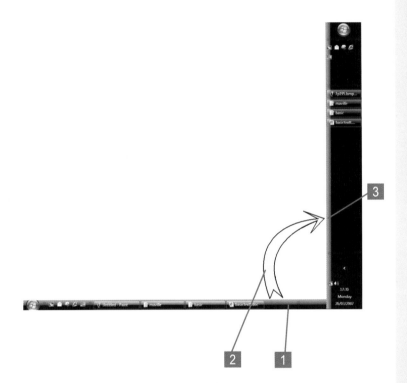

To move the Taskbar

1 Point to any free space on the Taskbar.

2 Drag towards the top, left or right of the screen, as desired.

3 Release the mouse button.

To resize the Taskbar

4 Point to the inside edge of the Taskbar.

5 When the cursor changes to ↔, drag to change the width of the Taskbar.

Timesaver tip

If you like to keep the Taskbar visible, it takes least space at the top or bottom of the screen.

If you have a lot of applications running at once, or several toolbars on the Taskbar, then the Taskbar is best at the left or right edge, but with Auto-Hide turned on.

Using Taskbar toolbars

Taskbar toolbars are sets of buttons which live on the Taskbar. Normally the Taskbar will have only the Quick Launch and the Language bars, apart from the buttons for any open applications and the clock.

If you find that you do not use them, these toolbars can be removed, to allow more space for application buttons.

If you like working from the Taskbar, other toolbars can be added, turning the Taskbar into the main starting point for all your commonly-used activities.

To add a toolbar

1 Right-click on an empty place on the Taskbar to open its context menu.

2 Point to Toolbars.

3 Click on a toolbar to add it to (or remove it from) the Taskbar.

To set toolbar options

4 Right-click on a toolbar to open its context menu.

5 Point to View and set the button size.

6 Turn on the toolbar Title if required.

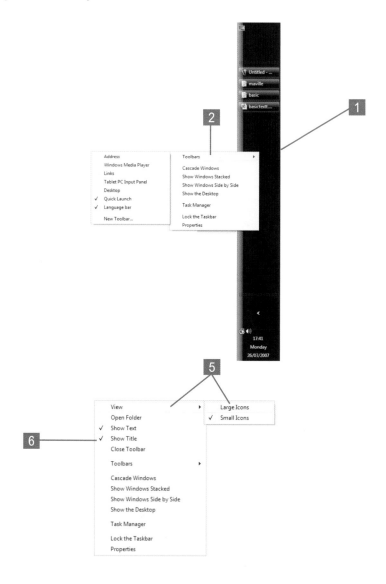

If you like the Taskbar as a means of starting programs, you can set up new Taskbar toolbars to hold your own collections of shortcuts to programs that you use regularly.

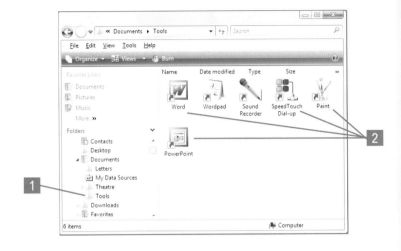

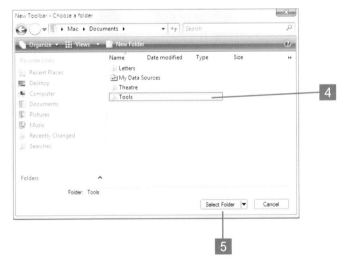

1 In Windows Explorer, create a new folder – it can be in any convenient place on your hard drive.

2 Set up shortcuts to your main programs.

3 Open the Taskbar menu, point to Toolbars and select New Toolbar.

4 Select your new folder.

5 Click Select Folder.

7

Important

If you add toolbars to the Taskbar, a horizontal display will get too crowded to see things properly unless you have it more than one line deep, as here. Otherwise, drag it to a side position, make it wide enough for the buttons to fit and turn on Auto-Hide.

Creating a user account

1 Click on the User Accounts and Family Safety link in the Control Panel.

2 Select Add or Remove user account.

3 Click Create a new account.

Windows Vista makes it easy for several people to share the use of one PC. Each user can have their own set of folders and their own customised Desktop and Start menu.

There are two types of account:

- Standard users have access to only their own files and those in the Shared Documents folder. They can customise their own desktops, and decide their own passwords and the pictures which identify their account.
- Administrators have full access to all aspects of the PC – including other users' areas.

You must have Administrator access to create accounts.

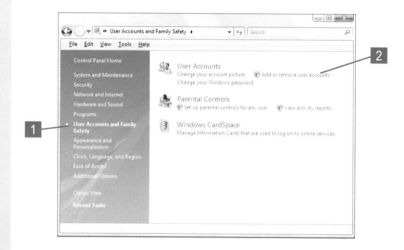

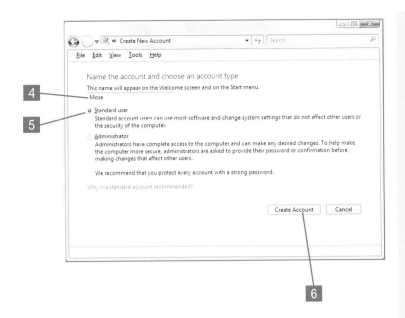

4 Enter the user's name and
click Next.

5 Set the account type.

6 Click Create Account.

Timesaver tip

Click Change the way users
log on and off, and make
sure that Fast User
Switching is enabled.

Important

Some older Windows
software may not run
properly with the Standard
account. Users who need
to run such applications
must be set as
Administrators.

Changing user details

Standard users can change only two aspects of their accounts: the password and the picture which appears on the welcome screen and Start menu. Administrator users can change all aspects of their own – or any other user's – account, including the account type. Changes can be made at any time.

1 Click the User Accounts and Family Safety link in the Control Panel. Administrators now need to pick the account.

To change the picture

2 Click Change your picture.

3 Select an image from the offered set or click Browse for more pictures to use one of your own files.

4 Click Change Picture.

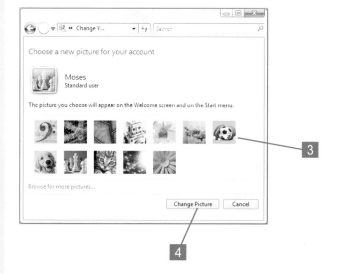

To add a password

5 Click Create a password for your account.

6 Enter the password twice – as you won't be able to read it, this is to check that you have typed it correctly.

7 Enter a hint to help you remember the password.

8 Click Create Password.

Important

Passwords can be a pain and should only be created if needed. If you do create one, click the Prevent a forgotten password link in the Related Tasks and create a 'password reset' disk. This will enable you to recover all your data should you later forget the password.

The password can be anything, but should be something that you can remember but that others are unlikely to guess. And the password hint should not be too obvious – it can be seen by other users.

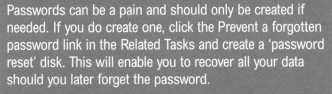

Jargon buster

.NET Passports – proof of identity that is accepted at many Internet sites that use secure systems to protect confidential data – set one up from here if you find that you need one.

Using the Character Map

This shows the full set of characters that are present in any given font, and allows you to select one or more individual characters for copying into other applications. Its main use is probably for picking up Wingdings for decoration, or the odd foreign letter or mathematical symbol in otherwise straight text.

The characters are rather small, but you can get a better look at a character by holding the mouse button down while you point at it. This produces an enlarged image.

1 On the Start menu, select All Programs then go to the Accessories menu and select Character Map.

2 Select the Font.

3 Click on a character to highlight it.

4 Click Select to place it into Characters to Copy.

5 Go back over Steps 3 and 4 as necessary.

6 Click Copy to copy to the Clipboard.

7 Return to your application and Paste the characters into it.

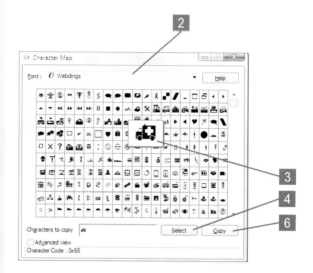

Did you know?

In Word, you can insert special characters directly using the Insert Symbol routine.

Gadgets are mini-applications that you can run in the Sidebar, on the right of your Desktop. Some are handy utilities, some show the latest news headlines, stock reports or weather forecasts from the Web, others are just for fun. All are worth exploring.

There are around a dozen gadgets supplied as part of the Vista package, and more available online. These can be added at any time – and removed again if you find that you do not use them.

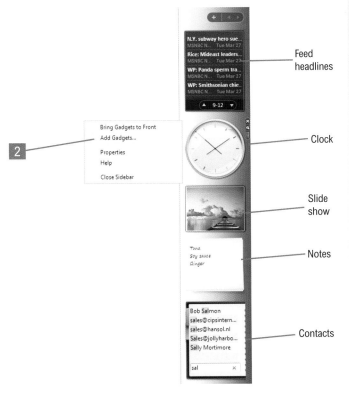

Feed headlines

Clock

Slide show

Notes

Contacts

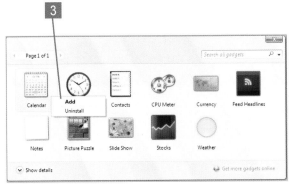

Adding gadgets

1. Right-click anywhere on the Sidebar.

2. Select Add Gadgets…

3. At the gadgets window, right-click on a gadget and select Add.

Timesaver tip

If the Sidebar is not visible, click the Sidebar icon in the Notification area.

7

Customising gadgets

Gadgets can be customised and/or controlled, but in different ways, depending upon what they are. Here is the clock, for example. You can change the face, name and the time zone. (You can have several clocks, each set to a different time zone, in which case the name could identify the location.)

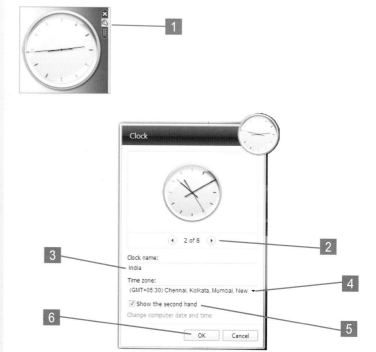

1 Point to the top right to get the toolbar and click the Options button – the Clock options dialogue box will appear.

2 Use the arrows to cycle through the choice of faces until you find the one you prefer.

3 If you have several clocks, type in a name to suit the location.

4 Select a time zone.

5 Tick the Show the second hand box, if it is wanted.

6 Click OK.

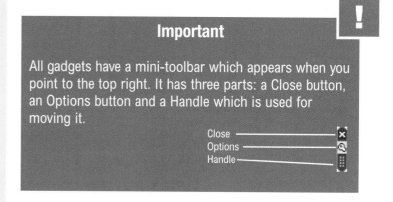

Important

All gadgets have a mini-toolbar which appears when you point to the top right. It has three parts: a Close button, an Options button and a Handle which is used for moving it.

Close
Options
Handle

The control options apply to all gadgets. Right-click on a gadget to display its menu of controls.

There are only half a dozen.

- Add Gadgets opens the Gadgets Gallery as we saw earlier.

- Detach from Sidebar – when a gadget is detached, it initially goes to the top left of the Desktop, though it can be dragged from there to anywhere on screen. Some gadgets become larger when detached – Calendar shows the month and the day, Slide Show, Feed Headlines and other information displays become twice the size.

- Move – selects the gadget so that you can move it within the Sidebar. To move it, drag on the handle.

- Opacity – gadgets can be distracting. If you reduce their opacity and make them more transparent, they are less eye-catching. When you point to one, it becomes solid once more.

- Options opens the Options dialogue box.

- Close Gadget removes the gadget from the Sidebar.

Did you know?

If you have an always-on broadband connection, the Feed Headlines gadget will bring up to the minute news to your desktop.

Looking after your PC

Introduction

A modern PC requires very little maintenance – and certainly very little physical maintenance. Wiping the screen with an anti-static cloth from time to time is about all that is normally necessary – if any component fails, there's little you could have done to prevent it, and nothing you can do to mend it (though replacement of most parts is very simple).

It's the hard disk, or rather, the data that is stored on the hard disk, which needs the maintenance. The more a disk is used, and the more data that is stored on it, the more necessary maintenance becomes. Look after your storage, and you should be able to enjoy many years of happy computing; neglect it, and one day you will find that some of your files have gone missing or become unreadable, and they may be essential and irreplaceable.

In this chapter you will learn how to keep your hard disk working efficiently, and how to back up files so that if the worst does happen and your hard disk fails, at least your data will be safe.

What you'll do

Find the System Tools

Check a disk for errors

Defragment a disk

Back up

Restore files from backups

Restore to a previous version

Clean up the hard disk

Remove programs

Change Windows components

Keep Windows up to date

Add a printer

Cancel a print job

Finding the system tools

These programs will help to keep your disks in good condition, and your data safe.

- Backup – enables you to keep safe copies of your important files, and to recover lost data.
- System Restore – backs up essential files, so that the system can be restored to normal after a crash.
- Disk Cleanup – finds and removes unused files.
- Disk Defragmenter – optimises the organisation of storage to maximise the disk's speed and efficiency.
- Error-check – finds and fixes errors in data stored on disks.
- Scheduled Tasks – lets you perform maintenance at set times.
- System Information – gives (technical) information about what's going on inside your computer.

Most of the tools can be started from the System and Maintenance part of the Control Panel; some are reached through the hard disk's Properties panel.

1. Click Start.
2. Select Control Panel.
3. Select System and Maintenance.
4. Click on a link to start a job.

The four system tools that are needed for the routine housekeeping can also be reached from the Properties box of any disk. The messages will remind you of chores you have been neglecting!

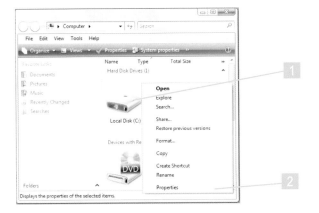

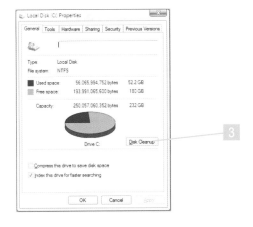

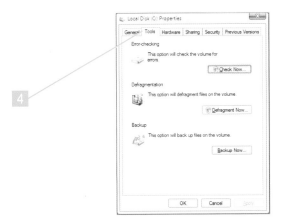

Finding the system tools (cont.)

1 Open Explorer, right-click on the drive for the context menu.

2 Select Properties.

3 Click Disk Cleanup.

or

4 Go to the Tools tab to start the Error-check, Defragmenter or Backup.

8

Checking a disk for errors

Data is stored on disks in *allocation units*. A small file may fit on a single unit, but others are spread over many. A file's units may be in a continuous run or scattered over the disk (see opposite), but they are all kept together by links from one to the next. Sometimes the links get corrupted leaving *lost fragments*, with no known links to any file, or *cross-linked files*, where two are chained to the same unit of data.

The magnetic surface of the disk may also (rarely) become corrupted, creating *bad sectors* where data cannot be stored.

The Error-checking routine can identify these and, with a bit of luck, retrieve any data written there and transfer it to a safe part of the disk. It is very simple to run, with only two options at the start, and nothing for you to do once it's running.

1 Go to the Tools tab of the disk's Properties dialog box and click [Check Now...].

2 For a quick check, turn off the options.

3 If you think the disk has errors, turn on one or other option.

4 Click [Start].

- With Automatically fix file system errors on, it will try to solve any problems that it meets – and it will do this better than you or I could, so leave it to it!
- Scan for and attempt recovery of bad sectors will test the surface of the disk, to make sure that files can be stored safely, and rebuild it if necessary. This automatically runs the first option.

If no option is set, the routine simply checks that the files are stored safely.

Microsoft Windows

Windows can't check the disk while it's in use

Do you want to check for hard disk errors the next time you start your computer?

[Schedule disk check] [Cancel]

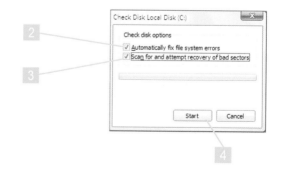

When you first start to write data onto a disk, the files are stored one after the other, with each occupying a continuous run of disk space. When you access one of these files, the drive simply finds the start point, then reads the data in a single sweep.

After the disk has been in use for some time, holes begin to appear in the layout, and not all files are stored in a continuous area. Some have been deleted, others will have grown during editing, so that they no longer fit in their original slot, but now have parts stored elsewhere on the disk. When you store a new file, there may not be a single space large enough for it, and it is stored in scattered sections. The drive is becoming *fragmented*. The data is still safe, but the access speed will suffer as the drive now has to hunt for each fragment of the file.

Disk Defragmenter should be run from time to time to pull scattered files together, so that they are stored in continuous blocks. It is best done on a regular schedule, at a time when the PC is not in use.

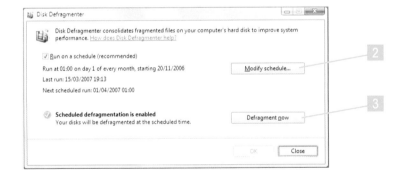

Defragmenting a disk

1 Run the Disk Defragmenter from the Control Panel or the disk's Properties box.

2 Click Modify schedule to set the time and frequency.

or

3 Click Defragment now to run it immediately.

8

Important

Defragmenting can take a while and will be even slower if you are using the PC at the time.

Backing up

1. On the Tools tab of the disk's Properties panel, click Backup Now... to run Backup Status and Configuration.

2. Click Change backup settings.

3. Put the backup CD/DVD into the drive.

Did you know?

A CD can store about 650 Mb of data – that's enough for three or four books like this, or hundreds of photos. For video storage, DVDs are a better bet. They can hold over 4.5 Gigabytes of data – the equivalent of seven CDs.

If program files are accidentally deleted, it is a nuisance but not a major problem as you can reinstall the application from the original disks. Data files are different. How much is your data worth to you? How long would it take you to rewrite that report or re-edit that image? Individual files can be copied onto floppies for safekeeping, but if you have more than one or two it is simpler to use Backup. A backup job is easily set up and will more than pay for itself in time and effort if you ever need it!

Backups are best done on CDs or DVDs. If you intend to back up large quantities of data regularly, invest £100 or so in an external hard drive so you don't have to struggle with a pile of disks.

The Backup routine is easy to use. To set it up, you specify the storage medium, types of files to be stored and the schedule. The first time that you run it, it will perform a complete backup of all the selected file types; in later backups, it will store only those that are new or have been changed.

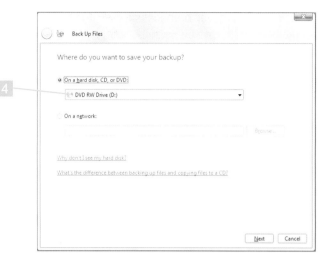

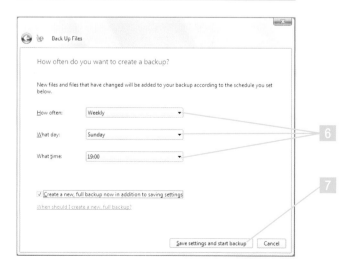

4 Select where the backup is to be stored. Notice that you can save on another PC if you are on a network. This may be convenient but is only really safe if the backup PC is in a different building.

5 Tick the types of files you want to store. You cannot select specific files or folders to include or ignore – all files of the selected types will be backed up.

6 Set the schedule, specifying how often, what day and what time. Backing up does not generally take that long, and is not that intrusive, but it will be done faster and more efficiently if you are not using the PC at the time.

7 Click Save settings and exit.

Restoring files from backups

With any luck this will never be necessary! But if you need to, it's a simple job.

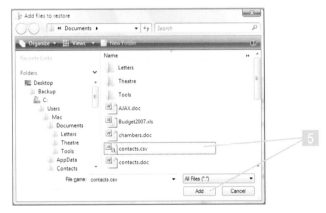

1. Run Backup Status and Configuration. Click the Restore Files button then select Restore Files in the main panel.

2. Insert the CD or DVD with the backup into its drive.

3. Click the Add files…

   or

4. Add folders… button.

5. Select the files and folders you want to restore and click Add.

6. Click Next.

7. Restore the file to its original location if you want to replace the existing file with the backup.

   or

8. Select a new location if you want to retain the current versions as well – there may be valuable data in the new file.

9. Click Start restore – that's it.

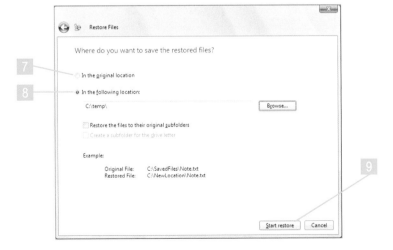

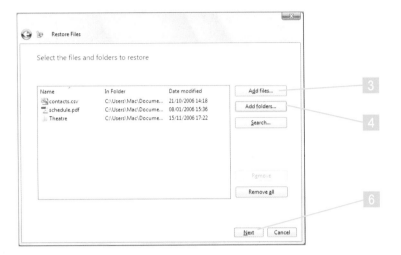

Even if you don't back up your files, Windows does. It automatically keeps 'shadow copies' of your files and folders as part of the system protection, and you can use these to revert to previous versions of files.

Restoring to a previous version

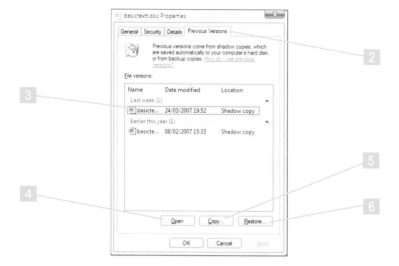

Run Windows Explorer and locate the file or folder that you want to recover. Right-click and select Properties from the context menu.

At the Properties panel, switch to the Previous Versions tab.

Find and select the copy from the last time when the file or folder was in the state you want it to be.

You have three choices:

Click Open to open a file for reading and resaving, or open a folder so that files can be selected for recovery.

or

Click Copy to copy the file or folder to a new location.

or

Click Restore to replace the original file or folder with the shadow copy.

Cleaning up the hard disk

Disk Cleanup is a neat little utility, and well worth running regularly – especially if you spend much time on the Internet. When you are surfing, your browser stores the files for the text, graphics and programs on the web pages that you visit. This makes sense, as it means that if you go back to a page (either in the same session or at a later date), the browser can redraw it from the files, rather than having to download the whole lot again. However, if you don't revisit sites much, you can build up a lot of unwanted clutter on your disk. You can empty this cache from within your browser, but Cleanup will also do it.

The Recycle Bin can be emptied directly, or as part of the Cleanup.

Programs often create temporary files, but do not always remove them. Cleanup will also tidy up after them.

1. Run Disk Cleanup from the Start menu or click Disk Cleanup on the disk's Properties panel.

2. After it has checked the system, the Cleanup panel opens. Select the areas to be cleaned.

3. Click [OK].

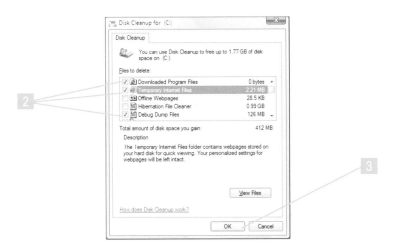

See also

If you really want to create some extra space on your system, check through your programs and the Windows Setup and remove any that you do not use. The More Options panel leads to the Add/Remove Programs routine – see the next page for more on this.

Installing new applications is easy nowadays – you just put the CD in the drive and follow the instructions! Removing unused programs is also easy – but you must do it properly, and not simply delete the application's folder in Windows Explorer. When applications are installed, entries are created in the Start menu, and files are associated with them. These all need to be removed as well. The Uninstall Programs routine will take care of all of this for you.

Removing Programs

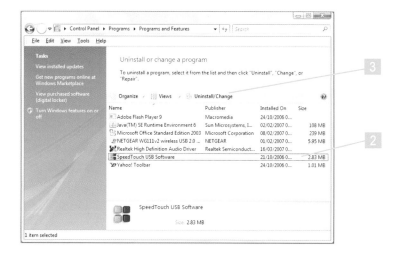

1 Open the Control Panel, select Programs then Uninstall a program.

2 Select the program.

3 Click Uninstall/Change .

4 You may be asked to confirm the removal of files that may be used by other programs – if in doubt, keep them.

5 Click OK .

Important

If data files have been stored in the program's folder, the routine will not be able to remove them – use Computer/Windows Explorer to tidy up any remnants.

Changing Windows components

Unwanted parts of Windows Vista can also be removed – and you can add accessories that were omitted during the initial installation.

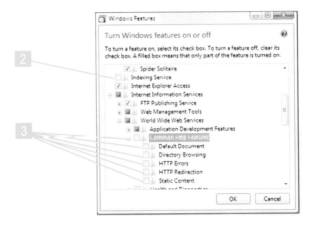

1. Open the Control Panel, select Programs then Turn Windows features on or off.

2. To remove an entire set of components, click on the checkbox to clear it.

3. To remove part of a set, click ⊞ to open the folder then clear individual check boxes.

4. When you have finished, click OK, wait while Windows reconfigures. It will take a few moments.

Timesaver tip

To add new accessories or other features, tick the checkboxes instead of clearing them!

Microsoft regularly produces improvements and bug-fixes for Windows, distributing them through the Internet. Windows has an Automatic Updates routine, which can connect regularly to Microsoft's site to get the latest patches and additions.

The Automatic Updates settings can be changed through the System and Maintenance item in the Control Panel. It can:

- Download automatically, notifying you when the files are ready to be installed.
- Alert you if it finds any new critical or optional updates.
- Be turned off completely, if you prefer to use the Windows Update link to check the site when it suits you.

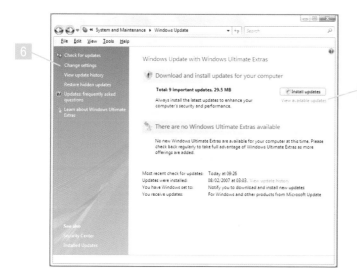

Keeping Windows up to date

1 Open the Control Panel and select System and Maintenance.

2 Select Windows Update.

To install updates manually

3 If you have chosen to control which updates are installed, and when, you will be told if updates are available. (You must be online so that the Update service can check the Microsoft website.) Click View available updates.

8

Keeping Windows up to date (cont.)

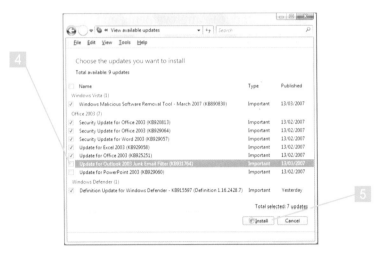

4 Clear the checkboxes for any updates that are not relevant to your PC.

5 Click Install.

To change your update settings

6 At the Windows Update window, select Change settings.

7 Select Install automatically, Download updates or Check for updates – you really should update one way or the other.

8 If you opt for automatic update, set the day and time to run the update.

9 Click OK.

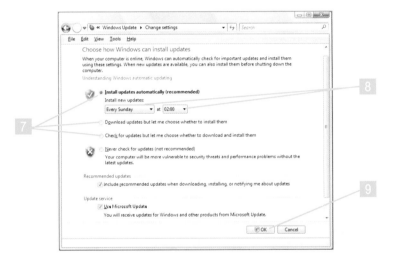

See also

See Chapter 9 to learn how to use Internet Explorer.

Important

After the files have been downloaded and installed, you normally have to restart the PC to bring thm into play, but it doesn't have to be done immediately – finish your session as usual. At the next start up, there will probably be a delay while your system files are updated.

If your printer is not detected and installed automatically by the plug and play technology, you can add it yourself easily. There is a wizard to take you through the steps, and Windows Vista has drivers for almost all but the most recent printers. If you have a very new machine, use the drivers on the printer's setup disk.

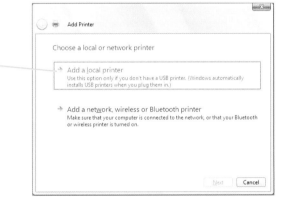

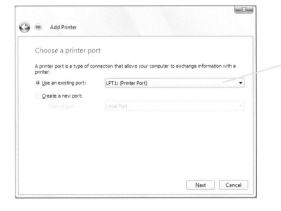

1 Open the Control Panel and select Printer in the Hardware section.

2 Click Add a printer on the toolbar to start the routine.

3 On a home machine, the printer is probably attached to your PC, so select Local.

4 Select the Port – normally LPT1.

8

Adding a printer (cont.)

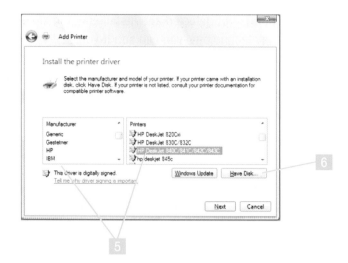

5 Pick the Manufacturer then the Printer from the lists.

or

6 Insert a disk with the printer driver and click Have Disk.

7 Change the name if you like – a networked printer should have a clear recognisable name to identify it.

8 Set the printer as the default if appropriate.

9 At the final stage opt for the test print, then click Finish and wait.

Jargon buster

Drivers – software that converts the formatting information from an application into the right codes for the printer.

When you send a document for printing, Windows Vista will happily handle it in the background. It prepares the file for the printer, stores it in a queue if the printer is already busy or offline, pushes the pages out one at a time and deletes the temporary files it has created. Nothing visible happens on screen – unless the printer runs out of paper or has other faults.

This is fine when things run smoothly, but they don't always when you are printing. You may run out of ink or paper part way through the job; you may decide that you don't like the look of the first page of a long document so that there is no point in printing the rest; and sometimes your PC and your printer will get their wires crossed for no discernable reason. If you need to cancel the printing of a document, it can be done.

Cancelling a print job

1 Open the Printers folder from the Control Panel, right-click on the active printer and select Open.

or

2 Right-click on the 🖶 icon in the Taskbar and select the printer.

3 Select the file(s).

4 Press [Delete] or open the Document menu and select Cancel.

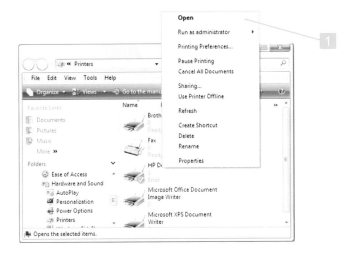

The Internet

9

Introduction

This chapter aims to introduce some of the basic concepts of and ways of working on the Internet, and explores just a few of its almost infinite possibilities. I've tried to keep things as simple as possible, which hasn't been that difficult for me because the key Internet activities are essentially quite simple. There are all sorts of refinements and alternative ways of achieving similar results, and there are a few complexities, but these can be ignored until you are ready to deal with them. Of course, this simplified approach does mean that if things go wrong – and they do from time to time – you may not know how to deal with it. But let's be positive. As long as you follow the instructions, you should be fine, and an hour or so from now, you should have visited dozens of websites and found out all sorts of interesting things.

The software that is used here is Internet Explorer. This is supplied as part of Windows, and is a powerful piece of software – easy to use but with all the sophisticated features that you need to get the best out of browsing the World Wide Web. Only the main features are covered here, but that is all you need to get started. The screenshots are from Internet Explorer 7.0, the latest version at the time of writing.

To use this chapter, you need to have an Internet connection already in place, or if you haven't got one of your own yet, you need to visit one of the kids or a friend, or go to the public library – somewhere that you can get online.

Jargon buster

Browser – application specially designed for accessing and displaying the information in the World Wide Web. This is also true the other way: the web is an information system designed to be viewed on browsers.

Email – electronic mail, a system for sending messages and files across networks.

HTML – HyperText Markup Language, a system of instructions that browsers can interpret to display text and images. HTML allows hypertext links to be built into web pages.

Net – short for Internet. And Internet is short for interlinked networks, which is what it is. (See Chapter 2 for more details.)

Page – or web page, a document displayed on the web. It may be plain or formatted text; and may hold pictures, sounds and videos.

Web – World Wide Web. Also shortened to WWW or W3.

Let's start by clearing up a common misconception. The 'web' and the 'Internet' are not the same thing. Some people use the terms interchangeably, but they shouldn't.

- The **Internet** is the underlying framework. It consists of the computers, large and small, that store and process information for the Internet; the telephone wire, network cable, microwave links and other connections between them; and the software systems that allow them all to interact.
- The **World Wide Web** is the most visible and one of the simplest and most popular ways of using the net. It consists of – literally – billions of web pages, which can be viewed through browsers, such as Internet Explorer. The pages are constructed using HTML, that tells browsers how to display text and images, and how to manage links between pages. Clicking on a hypertext link in a page tells the browser to go to the linked page (or sometimes to a different type of linked file) – wherever it may be.

Email is another simple and very popular use of the Internet, and there are other more specialised Internet activities, as you will see later in this book.

 Discovering the Internet and the web

9

Starting to browse

1 Click the Internet Explorer item at the top of the Start menu.

or

2 Double-click the Internet Explorer icon on the Desktop.

3 Wait a few moments for Internet Explorer to start.

4 If Internet Explorer is set to connect to a website when it first starts, then the Connection dialogue box will appear automatically. If it does not, double-click the desktop icon for your Internet connection. (This dial-up is Speedtouch, yours may well be different.)

5 The Connection dialogue box will have the User name already in place. The Password may also be there; if not type it in now.

6 Click [Connect].

7 Wait a few seconds.

Without further ado, let's go online and browse the World Wide Web. To do this you must first start Internet Explorer and connect to your Internet service provider.

You may find that when you start Internet Explorer, it will automatically try to make the connection. You may have to start the program and make the connection as two separate jobs. It all depends on your PC's setup – but either way, there's nothing difficult here, once you have located the icons on the Desktop or the Start menu.

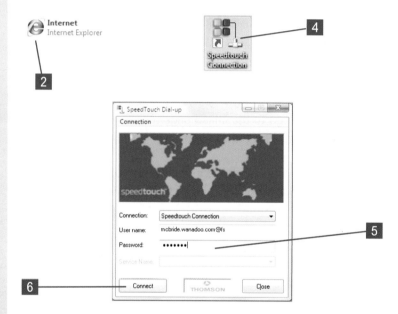

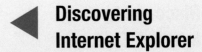

Discovering Internet Explorer

There are several optional elements to the Internet Explorer window, so yours may well not look like this at the moment – but it could! Try and identify as many features as you can.

Title bar   Address bar   Menu bar   Tabs   Search bar

toolbar handle

Links toolbar

Yahoo toolbar

Favorites Center

History list

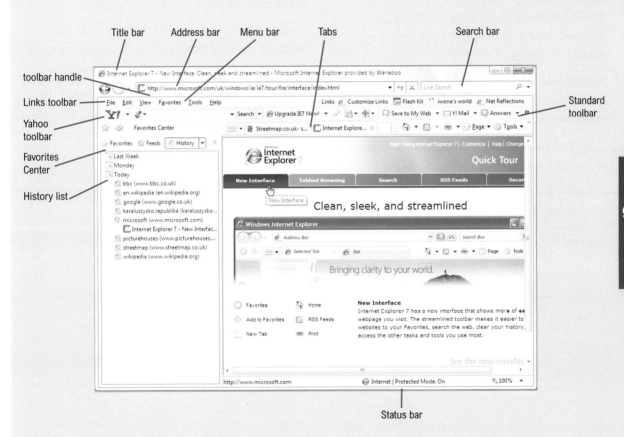

Standard toolbar

Status bar

9

Discovering
Internet Explorer
(cont.)

The toolbars

Title bar – shows the title of the web page, which is not the same as its URL.

Menu bar – gives you access to the full set of commands.

Standard toolbar – with tools for the most commonly-used commands. This and the Address and Links bars can be hidden if not wanted.

Address bar – shows the URL (Uniform Resource Locator, the address and filename) of the page. Addresses can be typed here.

Links toolbar – links to selected sites. There are predefined links to Microsoft's sites, but you can change these and add your own links.

Toolbar handles – you can drag these to move the toolbars.

Other features

Explorer bar – can be opened when it is needed to display your History (links to the places visited in the last few days) or your Favourites (links to selected pages), or to run a search for information. Clicking on a link in the Explorer bar will display its page in the main window.

Divider – click and drag on this to adjust the width of the Explorer bar. You may need more space when using the Explorer bar for a search.

Scroll bars – will appear on the right and at the bottom if a web page is too deep or too wide to fit into the window.

Status bar – shows the progress of incoming files for a page. When they have all downloaded, you'll see 'Done'. It also shows the address in a link when you point to it.

The navigation tools

Use these to move between the pages you have already visited during the session:

1 Back takes you to the page you have just left.

2 Forward reverses the Back movement.

3 The drop-down page list allows you to select from the last dozen or so pages.

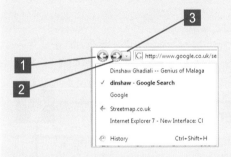

The standard toolbar

These buttons contain almost all of the controls that you need when you are online:

1 Home goes to your start page – your jumping off point into the web. This can be your own home page or any other.

2 Feeds are used to alert you to new content in web pages. Not all sites offer a feeds service – click the button when you are on a page to see if feeds are available from it.

3 Print prints the current page (text and graphics).

4 Page opens a menu. Its commands are related to the content of pages. Note these useful ones:

- Copy copies text or images for pasting into a document.
- Save As stores a copy of the page.
- Send Page/Link by Email connects you to Windows Mail to send someone the page, or a link to it.
- Zoom enlarges the text and graphics.
- Text size enlarges, or reduces, the text size.

5 Tools also leads to a menu. Its commands are more varied – key ones include:

- Pop-up Blocker: turn this on to block pop-up windows – usually carrying adverts – opening when you visit web pages.
- Phishing Filter should be turned on to restrict those emails that try to con you into giving out banking and other personal details.
- Full screen removes the toolbars and uses the entire screen to display a page.
- The Toolbars submenu controls the display of toolbars and sidebars.
- Internet Options allow you to configure Explorer to suit your needs.

9

Discovering Internet Explorer (cont.)

6 Help opens a menu offering alternative ways to get help.

7 Research opens the Research task pane.

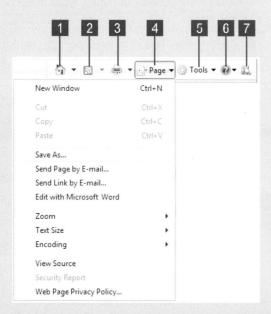

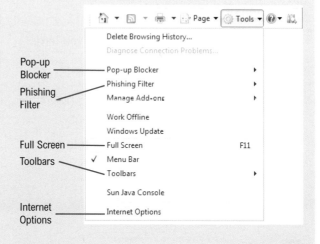

Pop-up Blocker

Phishing Filter

Full Screen

Toolbars

Internet Options

See also

See Using Favourites on page 239 and Viewing the History list on page 243 for more on these uses of the Explorer bar.

See Printing web pages on page 247 to find out about the Print options.

Timesaver tip

If you are having trouble downloading a web page, it may help to start again from scratch. Click Stop, then Refresh.

If you want to 'browse' the web, all you need is a good place to start, and one of the best places is a net directory – a site with sets of organised links to other sites. And one of the best directories is Yahoo! What makes it so useful is that it is extremely comprehensive, but all the sites listed there have been recommended by someone at some point. Quality control is rare on the web.

Browsing the web

1 Go to Yahoo! by typing this address into the Address bar: search.yahoo.com

2 Drop down the menu from the more link and select Directory.

Timesaver tip

If you know what you are looking for, you may find it more quickly by typing it in the Search field at the top of the page.

9

Browsing the web (cont.)

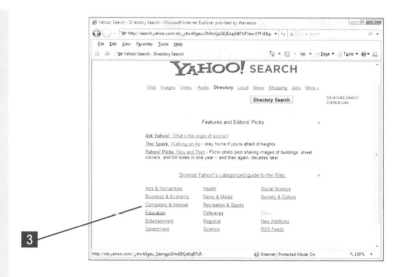

3 Think of a topic that interests you and in the web directory area click on the heading that the topic would fall under.

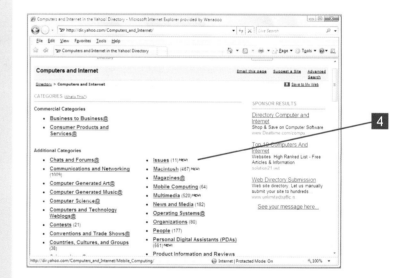

! Important

A hyperlink (link for short) is a connection to another web page. When you click on a link, Internet Explorer goes to that page and displays it. You know when you are on a link because the ⌖ pointer becomes a ⟨ᑭ hand.

When you are looking for material at Yahoo! don't worry too much if you are not sure which category your topic will fit into. The directory is so well cross-referenced that any reasonable start point should get you there.

The directory is organised as a hierarchy with many levels. At each level there are three sets of links:

- At the top are links to Categories – most of these are subdivisions of the current category; those with @ after the name are cross-links to other parts of the hierarchy.

- The second set are Sponsored links – i.e. to firms that have paid to be included.

- The third set are the Site listings.

As you work down through the levels, the first set shrinks, and the third set grows.

4 Use the category links to get down through two or three levels, to reach a specialised topic of your choice.

5 Click a Site listing link.

9

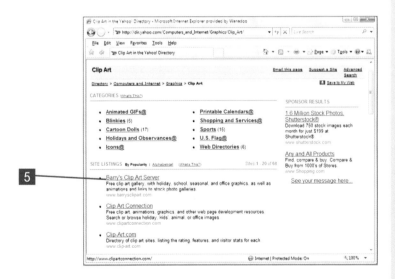

Browsing the web (cont.)

There's so much to see on the web! In fact, there's too much. You can often find links to scores – or even hundreds – of sites on a topic, so you have to learn to be selective or you can waste an awful lot of time online. Dip into a site to get an idea of what it is like, and if it's not really what you are looking for, move on and try elsewhere.

7 When the new page has loaded in, read to see if it is of interest. If you see a link that looks promising, click on it to find out where it leads.

8 If you want to go back to the previous page at the site, or back from there to Yahoo!, click .

9 If you want to start browsing a new topic, either work your way back to the start page in Yahoo!, or enter the search.yahoo.com address and start again from the top.

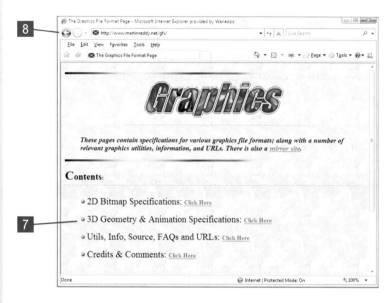

Important

Sometimes when you click on a link, the new page opens in a new window. This can be useful as it means that the previous page is still there in the original Internet Explorer window. However, there are a couple of catches. It can get a bit confusing if you have too many windows open at once, and the Back button only works within the same window. As a general rule, if a site has opened in a new window, close the window when you have finished with that site.

Web directories offer one approach to finding material on the web. Search engines offer another, and this is often the best way if you are looking for very specific information. A search engine is a site that has compiled an index to web pages, and which lets you search through the index. There are several dozen search engines, and they compile their indices in different ways and to different levels of completeness, but some of the best know what's on 80% or more of the pages on the web. The most complete and the most effective is Google. It is so well used and loved that searching the web is now often called 'googling'.

You search by giving one or more words to specify what you are looking for. Try to be specific. If you search for 'football', 'bridge' or 'gardening' you will get millions of links to possible pages.

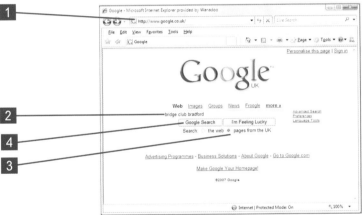

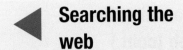

Searching the web

Search the web

1 Go to Google at: www.google.co.uk

2 Type in one or more words to describe what you would like to find, e.g. 'bayeux tapestry', or 'bridge club bradford'.

3 If you are looking for an organisation or supplier in the UK, or you want information about something UK-based, select the pages from the UK option.

4 Press the [Enter] key or click the Google Search button.

5 The results show the names and the first couple of lines of details from the matching pages. Scroll through to find the ones that look most promising.

6 Click on the page name link to go to the page.

7 Use ⬅ to return to Google if you want to follow up other links.

9

Searching the web (cont.)

Google has links to over 8 billion pages in its index! Which is why you have to be as specific as possible when looking for particular information. However, sometimes it pays to be less specific, as this can produce leads that you might never have thought of yourself.

It doesn't matter too much if you get millions of results from a search as the good stuff tends to be listed at the top. (Google has developed some very clever systems for rating pages.)

Important

You will find a link to the next page at the bottom of the results listing, but as a general rule, if you don't see anything useful in the first page, subsequent pages are unlikely to be any better. Try a new search instead, with different words.

A favourite is an address stored in an easily-managed list. To return to a favourite place, you simply click on it in the list.

Favourites can be accessed through the Favourites menu or through the Explorer bar. We'll start with the menu approach.

Using Favourites

1 Open the Favourites menu.

2 If the Favourite is in a folder, open its sub-menu.

3 Click on the one you want.

Did you know?

Even if you haven't yet added a Favourite of your own, there should be some already in the list – mainly to Microsoft's sites.

9

Adding a favourite

Internet addresses are a pain to type. One mistake and either you don't get there at all, or you find yourself at a totally unexpected site. (Try www.microsfot.com sometime.) Favourites are one way of being able to return to a site without having to retype its address.

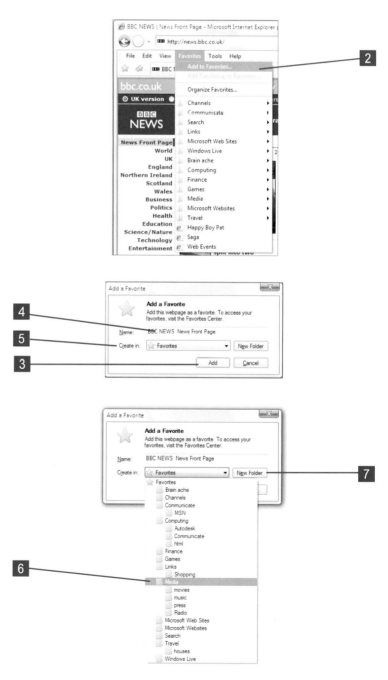

1 Find a good site!

2 Open the Favourites menu and click Add to Favourites.

3 The Add a Favourite dialogue box will open. Internet Explorer will have derived the Name from the page. If you are happy with the name and want to add the link to the main Favourites list, click [Add].

otherwise

4 Edit the suggested name, or type a new one – you want something that will work well as a menu item, so aim for short but meaningful.

5 To store it in a folder, click the Create in button to expand the folder list.

6 If there is a suitable folder, click on it.

7 If not, click [New Folder].

8 Type a name for the folder and click Create in.

9 Back at the Add a Favourite dialogue box, click [Add].

You can store your favourites in one simple list, but this soon gets unwieldy. If there are more than about twenty items, the menu takes up too much screen space and it can be hard to find the favourite you want. The solution is to organise your favourites into folders, which then become sub-menus in the Favourites system. It's easy to create new folders and to move entries into them.

Organising your Favourites

1 Click Organise Favourites on the Favourites menu.

2 Click New Folder .

3 A new folder will appear. Give it a suitable name.

4 Drag the link on to the folder and drop it in. If you pause over the folder first, it will open and you can then place the link exactly where you want it in the list.

or

5 Select the link and click Move... .

6 Select the folder from the list.

7 Click OK .

9

Using History

As you browse, each page is recorded in the History list as an Internet shortcut – i.e. a link to the page. Clicking the History button opens the History list in the Explorer bar. Click a link from here to go to the page.

If you are online at the time, Internet Explorer will connect to the page. If you are offline, it will display the page if all the necessary files are still available in the temporary Internet files folder, otherwise it will ask you to connect.

1. Click on the Favourites button.

2. Click on the History button in the favourites toolbar.

3. Click on the name to open the day and the site folders (if relevant in that view).

4. The Favourites pane will normally close after you have selected a link. If you want to keep it open, click the Pin button.

5. To close a folder, click on its name.

6. Click ⊠ to close the Explorer bar when you have finished.

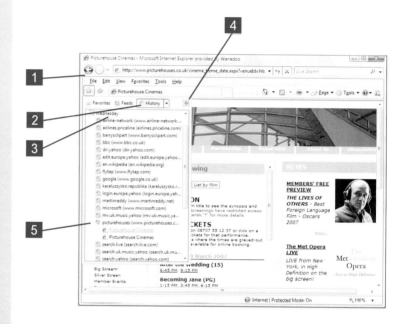

The History list can be viewed in four ways:

- By Date groups the links into folders by date and then by site. This is useful if you know when you were last there, but not the name of the site – and you may well not know where a page was if you reached it through a hyperlink.
- By Site groups the links into folders by site. This is probably the most convenient view most of the time.
- By Most Visited lists individual page links in the order that you visit them most. If there are search engines or directories that you regularly use as start points for browsing sessions, they will be up at the top of the list.
- By Order Visited Today lists the individual pages in simple time order. Use this view to backtrack past the links that are stored in the drop-down list of the Back button.

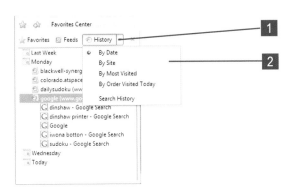

Viewing the History list

1 In the Explorer bar, click the History ▼ button to open the View menu.

2 Select the view which you think will enable you to find the required page fastest.

9

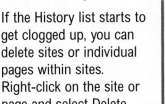

Timesaver tip

If the History list starts to get clogged up, you can delete sites or individual pages within sites. Right-click on the site or page and select Delete from the pop-up menu that appears.

Managing temporary Internet files

▶

When you visit a web page, the files that create it are downloaded onto your PC. These files are retained, and if you return to that page, either during the same session or later, it will then use the stored files, which is quicker than downloading them again. It also means that you can revisit pages offline.

You can set the amount of storage space to suit the way you surf and the size of your hard disk. If you have plenty of space and you tend to go back to sites a lot – perhaps following up a succession of links from one start point, or perhaps because you like to revisit sites offline – give yourself a big cache. If space is a problem, cut the cache right down. And if you need to free up the disk space, delete all the stored files.

You can also choose when Internet Explorer should check for newer versions of the stored pages. The 'Automatically' setting should do the job – this will check at the first visit in a session, but select the 'Every visit to the page' option if your favourite sites are fast-changing ones, e.g. news sites.

1 Use Tools, Internet Options… to open the dialogue box.

2 If you need to clear space on your disk quickly, click [Delete…].

3 In the Browsing History area, click [Settings].

4 Choose when to check for newer versions of stored pages.

5 Use the arrow buttons, or edit the numbers to set the amount of disk space.

6 Click [OK].

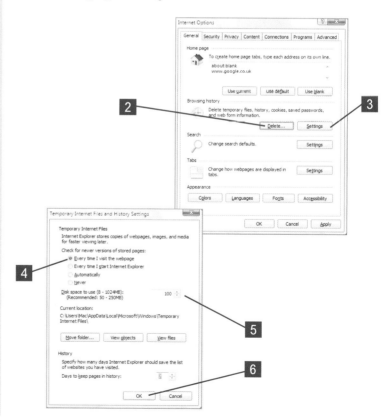

244

If you visit a lot of sites during your online sessions, and/or have set the number of days to keep the History links to a high value, then your History list could get very long. Beyond a certain point, its value as an aid to better browsing starts to diminish. You are probably best to set the days to no more than seven. The situations in which the History is most useful are those where you want to look back in leisurely offline time at pages that you glanced at while online, and you are most likely to do that either on the same day or within a couple of days. When you find sites that you will want to return to regularly, don't use the History – add them to your Favourites.

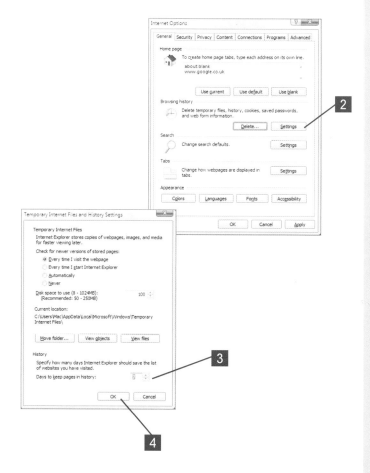

Controlling the History

1 Use Tools, Internet Options… to open the Internet Options dialogue box.

2 Click [Settings] in the Browsing History area.

3 Type a new value or use the arrows to adjust the number of days.

4 Click [OK] to save the change and exit.

Important

If you have been hunting for a special present or planning a surprise holiday, and don't want anyone to stumble on the sites, you can delete selected sites from the History list or click [Delete…] to completely wipe out your tracks (see above). Note that this will also erase the addresses stored in the Address.

9

Previewing before you print

A sheet of A4 paper and a computer screen are rather different shapes, and pages can be laid out on the screen in different ways. What this means is that you can never be entirely sure what a web page will look like when it is printed, or how many sheets it will be printed on – unless you use Print Preview. If the preview is acceptable, you can send it straight to the printer; if adjusting the layout might give a better printout, you can open the Page Setup dialogue box and change the settings.

Using Print Preview

1. Open the File menu and select Print Preview.

2. Use the arrows to work through the pages.

3. Change the Zoom level to look at details or the overall layout.

4. If you want to adjust the page layout, click the Page Setup button (see the next page for more on this).

5. To print the page(s), click 🖨.

6. To return to the normal web page display without printing, click ⨉.

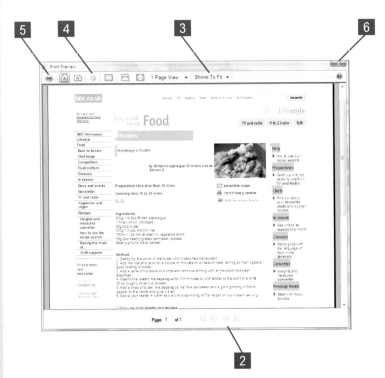

If you just want a printed copy of the whole of the current page, you simply click the Print button. Sometimes you need to control the printout – you may only want part of a long page or a section of a framed page, or you may want to print sideways on the paper (landscape orientation), or print several copies. In these cases, you need to go into the Print dialogue box.

Timesaver tip

You can sometimes get better results by copying part or all of a page into your word processor and printing it from there.

Important

The Print and Print Preview commands are also on the menu that drops down from the Print button.

Printing web pages

1 To print the current page, just as it is, click ▾.

2 If you only want to print part of a page, use the mouse to select it now – you may sometimes find that additional items get selected alongside the part that you wanted. That's just the way web pages are!

3 If the page is very long, open the File menu and select Print Preview, to see which printed pages you will want.

4 Open the File menu and select Print.

5 Select the pages, if relevant.

6 Set the number of copies.

7 Click on Print.

9

Installing add-ons

Browsers can display only formatted text and GIF and JPG graphics; but add-ons extend the range of files that they can handle. These are extensions to the browser, not independent applications. Some are present from the start, others can be downloaded from Microsoft or other sources when they are needed. Whenever you meet a file that needs an add-on, it will normally be accompanied by a link that you can use to get the software. Exactly what you have to do to download and install the add-on varies, though the process is almost always straightforward and there are usually clear instructions. Here, for example, is what happens when you install RealPlayer.

1 You will be alerted when you need an add-on, and you will be offered a link to a site from whence you can download it. Follow the link.

2 At the site, read the instructions. If there are different versions of the software, choose the one for your computer system.

3 Start the download. You will be asked if you want to run the software. Click [Run].

4 Pick a folder to store the file – use Documents or any folder that you can find again easily. Do not change the filename!

Important

With some add-ons you install them by saving a file, then running that installation file from Windows. Others, like Real, perform the installation automatically. In all cases, follow the prompts, and use your common sense.

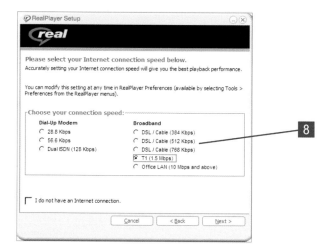

5 Wait while the file downloads. If you have a normal (56k) phone connection, this could take a while!

6 Installation will start automatically.

7 You will be asked to confirm the installation.

8 You will be asked to configure the software to your system. Set the options to suit, leaving at their defaults any that you do not understand.

9

Did you know?

Add-ons are almost always free. Their manufacturers make money by charging for the applications that create the files that the add-ons play.

Getting Adobe Reader ▶

Adobe Reader is one add-on that you really should have, as it is what you need to view and print PDF documents. People use PDFs for booklets and brochures, for books (this one went to the printer's as a PDF) and for paper sculpture kits (see the Did you know?) – in fact, for any document where well-formatted text and images are needed. PDF stands for Portable Document Format, and it is portable. A PDF file can be viewed on any computer or printed on any printer and the result will be the same.

1 When you try to open or download a PDF file you should find a link to get the Adobe Reader 'Plug-in'. Click it.

or

2 Head directly to Adobe at www.adobe.com and follow the links to get the Reader.

3 Follow the instructions to Download and install the Reader.

4 When you next come across a PDF file, Reader will start up inside Internet Explorer. Use its toolbar buttons to save, print or do other work with the document.

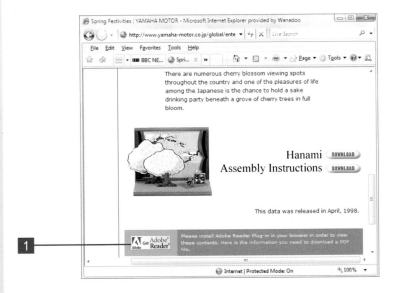

? Did you know?

Yamaha Motor Company have some lovely paper model kits (in PDFs) for free downloading – great for the grandkids on rainy afternoons! Find them at www.yamaha-motor.co.jp. Search for 'papercraft' and follow the links.

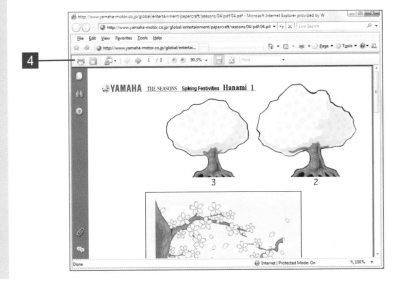

Some of you may have been working on someone else's connection while reading this chapter, so before we leave, let's have a look at how to get connected. It's not hard. When I first went online, in the late 1980s, getting connected required relatively expensive equipment and quite a lot of technical know-how – and there wasn't that much to do once you got online! Today, the costs are minimal, no technical knowledge is needed, and the online possibilities are amazing.

To get connected you need four things:

- A computer – any reasonably modern computer will do. It does not need to be state-of-the-art or top-of-the-range. If you are buying a new system, the cheapest Windows Vista PC will do the job, or even a second-hand Windows XP machine – as long as it is in good condition. Apple Macs are fine, and less susceptible to viruses (which are mainly written by Windows programmers), but they are more expensive to buy and there is less software available for Apples. Cost: under £400 for a desktop PC complete with Windows, Internet Explorer, Windows Mail, a word processor, and other entry-level but adequate software. Spend more only if you need a higher specification machine, or more sophisticated software for other uses.
- A modem – the device which links the computer to the phone line. You need a different type of modem for a dial-up connection down a normal phone line than for a broadband connection. Modern PCs are usually sold with a standard modem built-in, and so are ready for a dial-up connection. If you take the broadband alternative, a suitable modem will be supplied as part of the deal.
- A phone line – or more to the point, a phone socket within reach of the computer. If necessary, you can get extension phone leads at any good DIY store. Cost: £5–£10.
- An account with an Internet service provider – the company that will link you to the Internet and provide you with your email address and web space if you want to set up a site.

Getting connected

9

Getting connected (cont.)

How do I choose an ISP?

There are basically three types of ISP account.

- A broadband connection gives high-speed access to the internet. This uses the normal phone line, but the line has to be reconfigured at the exchange before it can be used. Not all local exchanges have this capacity, so the first thing to do is to check that broadband is available in your area. Broadband users can connect at the start of the day and leave it connected until they shut down – it costs nothing and causes no problems as the phone can be used for normal calls while the computer is online.

  There are several variables: speed, download limits, number of email addresses that you can run from one account, and whether or not you are given web space. The cost will vary to match, from around £15 to £30 a month. You only need the very high speeds and high download limits if you intend to download a lot of music or videos. All broadband ISPs offer a free modem, but you must sign up for a minimum of 1 year.

  Broadband providers include AOL, Orange, BTInternet, Virgin and most other phone companies.

- A monthly contract dial-up account. This will work on any phone line – you can even connect through a mobile if you have a suitable lead. Though far slower than broadband, dial-up is what we all managed with perfectly happily until recently. Expect to pay £15 a month, and to get unlimited access on an 0800 line.
- A pay-as-you-go dial-up account. These also run on the standard phone line. They typically cost 1p per minute, with the charging done through your phone bill as the connections are to 0844 or 0845 numbers. If you mainly use the Internet for email, with occasional dips into the web to look things up, then pay-as-you-go can be an economic solution – one brief phone call a day to collect and receive your email should add up to a little over £1 a month. Dial-up account providers include AOL, Orange and many smaller firms, including my own excellent TCP.

The problem is, you don't really know what you need until you have been active online for a while. So here's a suggestion. Several ISPs – notably AOL – offer a free month's trial of their dial-up service. Try it. See how you get on, and make an informed decision at the end of the month.

9

Email

Introduction

The World Wide Web may well be the most glamorous aspect of the Internet and the one that grabs newcomers, but email is the aspect that many people find the most useful in the long run. It is quick, reliable and simple to use.

- Email is quick. When you send a message to someone, it will normally reach their mailbox within minutes – and usually within half an hour. However, it will only be read when the recipient collects the mail, and that may be anything from a few minutes later to when they get back from holiday.
- Email is reliable. As long as you have the address right, the message is almost certain to get through. And on those rare occasions when it doesn't, you will usually get it back with an 'undeliverable' note attached.
- Email is simple to use. You can learn the essential skills in minutes – as you will see very shortly!

Understanding email

It may help you to have an overview of the technology behind email, so you can use it more efficiently and are less likely to get fazed when things don't quite go according to plan!

When you send an email message, it does not go direct to your recipient, as a phone call does. Instead it will travel through perhaps a dozen or more computers before arriving at its destination – in the same way that snail mail passes through several post offices and depots. The message goes first to the mail server at your ISP. This will work out which computer to send it to, to help it towards its destination. The server will normally hold the message briefly, while it assembles a handful of messages to send to the next place – in the same way that the Post Office sorts and bags its mail. Each mail server along the way will do the same thing, bundling the message with others heading in the same direction. This method gives more efficient Internet traffic and at the cost of very little delay – most messages will normally be delivered in less than an hour.

However, your recipients won't necessarily be reading the message within the hour. The delivery is to their mail boxes at their service providers. People only get their email when they go online to collect it. (Though with a broadband account and automated collection it can feel as if its delivered.)

Email messages are sent as text files. A plain text message will normally be very short, as it takes only one byte to represent a character – (plus about 10% more for error-checking). A ten-line message, for example, will make a file of around 1 Kb, and that can be transmitted in about 3 seconds. Images, video clips and other files can be sent by mail (see page 270) but they must first be converted into text format. You don't need to worry about how this is done, as Windows Mail will do all the conversion automatically. What you do need to know is that conversion increases the size of files by around 50%, so even quite small images can significantly increase the time it takes to send or receive messages.

Jargon buster

Error-checking – the techniques used to make sure that data sent over the internet arrives intact. If a block of data is damaged, it is sent again.

Jargon buster

ISP (Internet service provider) – the company that supplies your connection to the Internet.

Jargon buster

Mail server – computer that stores and handles email.

Jargon buster

Plain text – text without any layout or font formatting

Windows Mail is the email software supplied with Vista. It is very simple to use – you can pick up your mail with one click of a button, and though it takes a little more to send a message, there's nothing complicated in it.

Views bar

Folder bar

Folder list

Headers pane

Preview pane header

Preview pane

Status bar

1 Start Windows Mail from the Start menu.

2 Identify the marked areas. If you are working on a friend's PC, check before you read any messages! If it's your own PC, and the software has been installed recently, you should have a welcome message from Microsoft.

Jargon buster

Snail mail – post hand-delivered by the postman.

10

Starting Windows Mail (cont.)

The three key elements of the Windows Mail window are the Folder list, the Headers pane and the Preview pane. There are another six elements that can be included in the display. Apart from the Headers pane, every element is optional and can be easily switched off if you decide that you do not want it.

■ The Headers pane is the only part of the display which is not optional, but even here you can control the layout and which items are displayed.

■ The Folder list shows your email and news folders. New email folders can be created if needed, and newsgroup folders are created automatically when you subscribe to groups. The contents of the current folder are displayed in the Headers area.

■ The Preview pane displays the current message from the Headers area. If this pane is turned off, messages are displayed in a new window. The pane can sit below or beside the Headers – below is usually more convenient.

■ The Views bar lets you switch between displaying all messages and those you have not yet read. The options are also available on the View menu.

■ The Folder bar shows the name of the current folder.

■ The Preview pane header repeats the From and Subject details from the Headers area.

- The Status bar, as always, helps to keep you informed of what's going on. Amongst other things, it tells you how many messages are in a folder, and shows the addresses behind hyperlinks in emails.

10

Exploring the commands

Windows Mail has a lot of commands that most of us will rarely use, and if you don't join the newsgroups, there are some that you will never use at all. In practice, the commands that you will use regularly can be found on buttons on the toolbar.

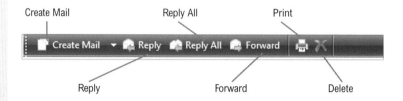

Create Mail

Click this button to start a new message in plain text or with the default formatting, or click the arrow to open a drop-down list.

Reply

Starts a new message to the sender of the current message – the same as Reply to Sender on the Message menu.

Reply All

Sends a reply to all the people who had copies of the message – the same as Message, Reply to All.

Forward

Copies the message into the New Message window, ready for you to send it on to another person, adding your own comments if you like. The same as Message, Forward.

Print

Prints the current message, using the default printer settings.

Delete

Deletion is a two-stage process. Clicking this button transfers the selected message(s) to the Deleted Items folder. Messages are then deleted from there when you close Windows Mail or when you delete them from the Deleted Items folder.

The full set of commands can be reached through the menus. These in particular are worth noting. The first two are on the Tools menu; Find is on the Edit menu.

Send/Receive

Sends anything sitting in the Outbox and picks up any new mail. If there's something in your Outbox that you do not want to send yet, e.g. a message with a big attachment that will take a long time to send, open the Tools menu and use Receive All instead.

Similarly, if you are in a hurry to send a message but do not have time to deal with incoming mail, you can use Tools, Send All.

Addresses

Opens your Address Book, to add a new contact, or to manage existing ones.

Find

Searches through your stored messages, on the basis of the sender, subject, text within the message, date or other factors.

Exploring the commands (cont.)

10

Reading an email message

Unlike snail mail, email does not get delivered directly to you. Instead, it goes into a mailbox at the provider and you must go online to get it. You can set Windows Mail to check for new mail automatically on start-up and/or at regular intervals while you are online, or you can pick up your mail when you feel like it.

When messages arrive, they are dropped into the Inbox folder. Opening them for reading is very straightforward. After reading, you can reply if you like, and the message can be deleted or you can move them to another folder – you might want to keep some for future reference. You can also just leave the message in the Inbox for the time being.

1 Start Windows Mail.

2 If you are not online already, get connected now.

3 From the Tools menu select Send and Receive, then Send and Receive All. Wait while the messages come in.

4 Select Inbox in the Folder list, if necessary.

5 Click anywhere on a message's line in the Header pane to open the message in the Preview pane. After reading the message...

6 If you don't want it any more, click ⊠.

7 If you want to leave it in the Inbox for the time being, click on the header line of the next message to read that.

8 If you want to respond to it, click 🔁 Reply.

Windows Contacts isn't just a convenience, it is also an essential tool for email. Addresses are rarely easy to remember and if you get just one letter wrong, the message won't get through. But if an address is stored in your Contacts, you can pick it from there whenever you need it.

Addresses can be added to the Contacts in two ways: you can type them in directly, or if you are replying to people who have written to you, you can get Windows Mail to copy their addresses into the Contacts.

Adding an address to Windows Contacts

1 Open the Tools menu and select Windows Contacts.

2 When the Contacts opens, click the New Contact button.

3 Type in the person's name, splitting it into First, Middle and Last – the separate parts can be used for sorting the list. You can miss out any part you don't need, or put the whole name into one slot.

4 Add a brief Nickname if you like – this can be used for selecting addresses later.

5 Type the address in the Email addresses slot, then click
    Add .

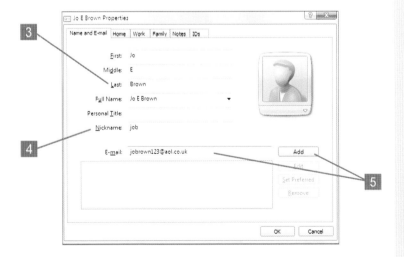

10

Adding an address to Windows Contacts (cont.)

The Contacts can store more than just email addresses. You can also add other contact information – home and business addresses and phone numbers – whatever is relevant; there is also space for the names of your contact's spouse and children, and even their birthday and anniversary dates. How much you put here is entirely up to you.

6 Switch to the Home or Work tab if you want to store the snail mail address or phone number.

7 Switch to the Family tab if you want to add family details or dates to remember.

8 Click [Add].

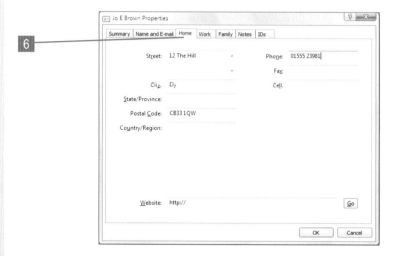

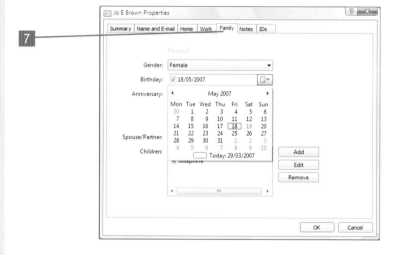

If there are only a couple of dozen entries in your Contacts, you should be able to find a person simply by scrolling through the list. As the numbers rise, it can take longer to spot the entry that you need. Searching is the answer.

If you type a few letters of the name into the Search box, Contacts will filter the list to display only the names that match. The more of the name that you type, the more the displayed set will shrink.

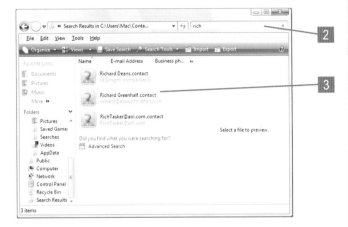

Finding a contact

1. If Contacts is not active, open the Tools menu and select Windows Contacts.

2. Type the first few letters – or any part of the name – into the Search box at the top right of the window.

3. Check the display as it is filtered, to see if the entry has been found.

4. Type more of the name if necessary.

Timesaver tip

Sometimes, email addresses will go into the Contacts list without their matching real names. If the email address bears no resemblance to their real name – and it happens – then the search will be more difficult. Try to remember something of the address, or of the company that the person works for, and search on that.

10

Writing a message

Messages are written in the New Message window. The main part of this is the writing area, but in the top part of the window there are several boxes which must be attended to.

- To: is the address of the recipient(s).
- Cc: (carbon copy) is for the addresses of those people, if any, to whom you want to send copies.
- You can also have Bcc: (blind carbon copy) recipients if you select their names from the Select Recipients dialogue box. These people will not be listed, as the To and Cc recipients will be, at the top of the message.
- Subject: a few words outlining the nature of your message, so that your recipients know what's coming.

1. Open the File menu, point to New and select Mail Message or click Create Mail.

2. Click To: to open the Select Recipients dialogue box.

3. Select a contact and click To: ->, Cc: -> or Bcc: ->, to copy the name into the recipient box.

   Repeat Step 3 if you want to add more recipients.

4. Click OK to return to the New Message window.

5. Enter a Subject for the message.

6. Type the message.

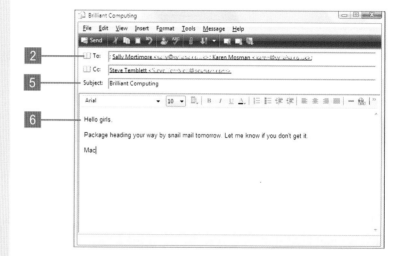

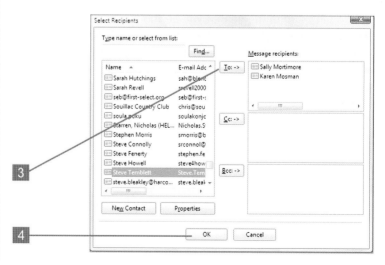

A message can be sent immediately after it has been written, or stored in the Outbox to be sent later. If you have a broadband connection, you would normally be online while you are writing the messages, and would send messages immediately. If you connect through the normal phone line, being online ties up the phone and (probably) costs money. In this case, you would be better to write your messages offline, store them in the Outbox then send all the new ones in one batch.

You can set the options so that either the Send button will send immediately or it will store messages. If you want to handle a message differently, there are Send and Send Later commands.

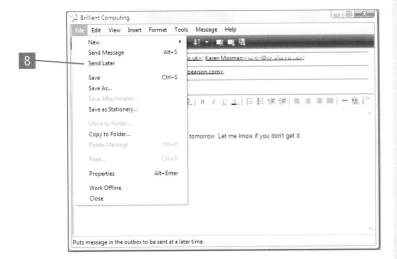

7 Click to use the default Send option.

or

8 Open the File menu and select Send Message or Send Later.

9 When you have finished all your writing, if there are messages in the Outbox, open the Tools menu, point to Send and Receive and select Send All. If you aren't online, the Connect dialogue box will appear, ready to connect to your ISP.

Timesaver tip

If you forget to send the messages in the Outbox, Windows Mail will prompt you to send them before closing down. And if you close down without sending them, it will prompt you again the next time that you start Windows Mail.

10

Replying to an email

Replying to someone else's email is the simplest and most reliable way to send a message, because the address is already there for you.

When you start to reply, the original text may be copied into your message. You can decide whether or not this should happen, and how the copied text is to be displayed – these are controlled from the Tools, Options dialogue box. For the moment, go with the default settings.

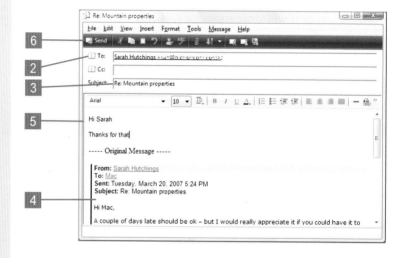

1 When you click **Reply** the Compose window will open.

2 The To: field will already have the email address in it – though it may actually display the person's name. Don't worry about that.

3 The Subject: field will have the original Subject text, preceded by 'Re:'. Edit this if you like.

4 The message area may have the original text copied in. You can edit or delete this if you like.

5 Add you own message.

6 Click **Send**.

If someone sends you a message that you would like to share with other people, you can do this easily by forwarding. The subject and message are copied into the New Message window, so all you have to do is add the address of the recipients and any comments of your own.

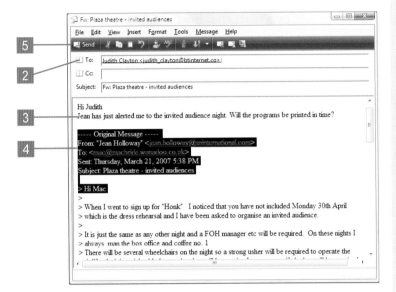

1. Select the message and click Forward.

2. Add the To: address.

3. Add any comments of your own.

4. Trim out any unwanted material from the original.

5. Click Send.

10

Attaching a file to a message

Images, documents, music, programs and other non-text files can be sent by email, attached to messages. As the mail system was designed for transmitting plain text, other files have to be converted to text for transfer, and back to binary on receipt. Windows Mail handles these conversions for you, but you need to be aware of the conversion, because it increases the size of files by about 50%. Big files get even bigger.

1. Start a new message as usual.

2. Open the Insert menu and select File Attachment... or click .

3. The standard Open dialogue box will appear. If you are looking for a picture, it may help if you switch to Large Icons view.

4. Locate and select the file, then click Open .

5. The file will be listed in a new Attach slot beneath the Subject line. Complete the message.

6. Click Send and wait – it takes a few moments for the system to convert the file.

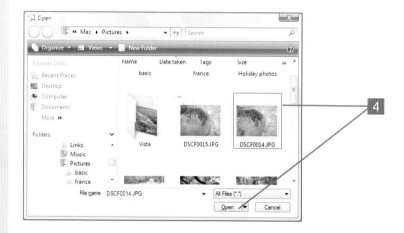

Important

If you have a dial-up connection, very large attached files can be a problem. If the connection is broken during transmission, you have to start sending or receiving again from scratch, and messages are sent in the order in which they are created or arrive in your mailbox – so a big file will block your communications until it gets through. And remember that this also applies to the people to whom you are sending messages – don't send people big files unless they want them!

You'll know if an incoming message has an attachment as there will be a little paperclip icon beside it in the header list. If you have opted to show the Preview pane header, you will also find a larger clip icon there.

For this next exercise you need a message with an attached file. So, you can either wait until someone sends you one, or you can attach a file to a message, set it to send later – so that it is in the Outbox – and then open the message. (And don't forget to delete it later if you only created the message to test the procedure!)

Saving an attached file

1 Open the message.

2 If the Preview pane header is present, click the paperclip icon and select Save Attachments.

otherwise

3 Open the File menu and select Save Attachments.

4 Locate the folder in which to store the file, then click Save.

Timesaver tip

If a picture has been attached to an HTML formatted message, you will be able to see it. Right-click on it and select the Save Picture As… command – it's exactly the same technique as you would use for capturing an image of a web page.

10

Opening an attachment

You can open an attachment directly from a message, without saving it. But take care. Some very nasty viruses are spread through email attachments. You get a message, apparently from an acquaintance, and when you open it, the virus program is executed. Typically, it will go through your address book, sending virus-laden messages to your contacts, and it may also destroy the files on the hard drive.

Any executable file (program) may be a virus. Common extensions for executable files include: .exe, .com, .bat, .vbx. Viruses can also be hidden in macros – programs that run within applications. These can be a problem in Word, Excel and PowerPoint. If you have any of these, make sure that they are set for high security in respect of macros. Go to the Tools menu, point to Macros, select Security… and set the level to High.

1 Open the message.

2 If the Preview pane header is present, click the paperclip icon and select the name of the attachment.

otherwise

3 Double-click on the message to open it in its own window, then right-click on the filename in the Attach line and select Open.

4 At the Mail Attachment dialogue box, think again and if you have any doubts about the file's safety, click ☐ Cancel ☐.

5 If you are confident that it is safe, click ☐ Open ☐.

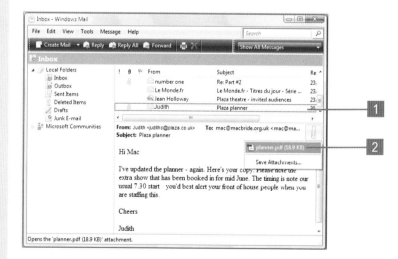

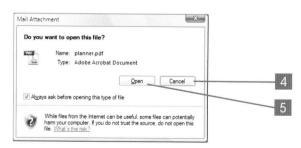

Important

!

Never open an executable file unless you have been expecting it and are absolutely certain that it is safe.

There are several ways in which you can customise your display. The first of these is to select the screen elements that you want to include in the layout. This is done in the Window Layout Properties dialogue box. Simply tick or clear the ticks to turn elements on and off.

1. Open the View menu and select Layout.

2. In the Basic area, click on the check boxes to turn an element on or off.

3. Click Apply to see the effect of your changes.

4. Go back to step 2 if you don't like the new layout.

5. Click OK to return to Windows Mail, or leave the dialogue box open and read on…

Important

The only elements that you really need are the Folder List – to move between your folders – and the Toolbar (unless you prefer to work from the menus).

10

Controlling the Preview pane

The Preview pane is optional – a message can also be opened into its own window. If the pane is present, it automatically displays whatever message is selected in the Headers pane. This can be useful, but it can also be a cause of problems – it all depends on how good the filters are at your Internet service provider. If they are filtering out the spam and those messages that contain viruses, then the Preview pane can be used safely. If not, turn the pane off so that you control which messages are opened.

1. Open the View menu and select Layout… to open the Window Layout Properties dialogue box.

2. In the Preview pane area, click the checkbox to turn the pane on or off.

   If the pane is on…

3. Select where the pane is to go – below is generally better as you can normally read the whole width of the message without scrolling the display.

4. Turn on the Preview pane header if you want it – it simply repeats the From and Subject information from the Headers pane.

5. Click [OK].

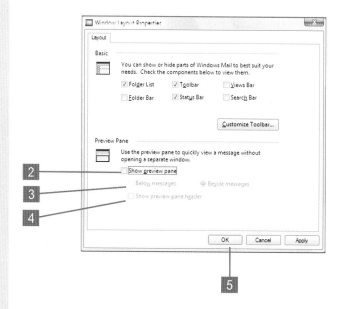

Jargon buster

Branch – in file management, the structure of sub-folders that opens off from a folder.

Browser – application specially designed for accessing and displaying the information in the World Wide Web. This is also true the other way: the web is an information system designed to be viewed on browsers.

Child folder – in file management, a sub-folder of a Parent.

Clipboard – windows has a special part of memory known as the Clipboard, which can be used for storing any kind of data – text, images, spreadsheets, complete files or small selected chunks. It can be used not just for copying or moving data within an application, but also between applications as the Clipboard can be accessed from any program.

Document – Windows uses 'document' to mean any file created by any application. A word-processed report is obviously a document, but so is a picture file from a graphics package, a data file from a spreadsheet, a video clip, sound file – in fact, any file produced by any program.

Driver – software that handles the interaction between the computer and a peripheral device. A printer driver converts the formatting information from an application into the right codes for the printer.

Email – electronic mail, a system for sending messages and files across networks.

Error-checking – the techniques used to make sure that data sent over the internet arrives intact. If a block of data is damaged, it is sent again.

Freeware – software ranging from well-meaning efforts of amateurs through to highly professional products like Acrobat Reader and Flash Player, which is given away so that people can view the documents and files created by paid-for applications.

GUI – Graphical User Interface – the screen display for an operating system such as Windows, that uses images, icons and menus. Users start operations and make choices by clicking on these, rather than having to type in command words.

HTML – HyperText Markup Language, a system of instructions that browsers can interpret to display text and images. HTML allows hypertext links to be built into web pages.

ISP – Internet Service Provider – the company that supplies your connection to the Internet.

Keyword – a keyword can be any word which might occur in the pages that you are looking for. If you give two or more, the system will only list pages which contain all those words.

Mail server – a computer that stores and handles email, either within a large organisation or at an ISP.

Net – short for Internet. And Internet is short for interlinked networks, which is what it is.

.Net passports – proof of identity that is accepted at many internet sites that use secure systems to protect confidential data – set one up from the User Accounts facility if you find that you need one.

Page – or web page, a document displayed on the web. It may be plain or formatted text; and may hold pictures, sounds and videos.

Parent folder – in file management, a folder that contains another.

Plain text – text without any layout or font formatting.

Root – in file management, the folder of the disk. All other folders branch off from the root.

Shareware program – a program supplied on a try-before-you-buy basis. At the end of the trial period, you can continue to use the program for a small fee, typically £10 to £20. Shareware programs include the excellent WinZIP file compression software, and Paint Shop Pro, a fully-equipped image editing and creation package.

Snail mail – mail that is hand-delivered by the postman.

Template – document that has formatting and layout in place ready for your text. It may have some text and images in place already, e.g. headed paper for letters.

Web – the World Wide Web, also shortened to WWW or W3.

Troubleshooting guide

The Internet

Working with text

New! Features

Microsoft Windows Vista

Microsoft Windows Vista has a brand new user interface that makes it easier and faster to use than earlier versions of Windows. Tasks such as opening and closing applications, searching for files and changing settings have been streamlined. New and improved programs have been developed to help you manage and store pictures, send and receive emails, browse the Internet, backup your data and stay secure. And the flexible new interface allows you to customise toolbars and optimise your working environment using Sidebars and Gadgets.

What's New?

The **New!** icon in the table of contents highlights the sections that have been significantly revised to demonstrate how tasks are carried out in the new Vista operating system. The following lists all the significantly revised and new sections and their location in the book.